# UNCONQUERED

## 10 PRINCIPLES TO OVERCOME
## ADVERSITY AND LIVE ABOVE DEFEAT

# ADAM DAVIS

**BroadStreet**
P U B L I S H I N G

BroadStreet Publishing® Group, LLC
Savage, Minnesota, USA
BroadStreetPublishing.com

Unconquered: 10 Principles to Overcome Adversity
and Live above Defeat
Copyright © 2023 Adam Davis

9781424565320 (softcover)
9781424565337 (ebook)

Stock or custom editions of BroadStreet Publishing titles may be
purchased in bulk for educational, business, ministry, fundraising,
or sales promotional use. For information, please email
orders@broadstreetpublishing.com.

Cover and interior by Garborg Design Works | garborgdesign.com

Printed in China

23 24 25 26 27 5 4 3 2 1

# DEDICATION

To every man and woman who has silently carried the pain of childhood abuse of any kind;

to every man and woman who lost the will to live, but still you fight;

to every man and woman who has lost a loved one to suicide;

to those who continue to battle their demons;

this book is for you.

Fight like hell.

Live unconquered.

This book contains material regarding sexual abuse and suicidal ideation and is not intended as a substitute for the medical advice of licensed therapists or physicians. You should regularly consult a medical professional in matters relating to your mental and physical health needs. If at any time you find yourself wrestling with suicidal thoughts, contact the 988 Suicide and Crisis Lifeline at 988.

# CONTENTS

# FOREWORD BY
# MARCUS LUTTRELL

I first met Adam in early 2019 when Lt. Col. Dave Grossman recommended that he be a guest on my podcast, *Team Never Quit*, shortly after the release of their book *Bulletproof Marriage: A 90-Day Devotional*. From the time I met Adam during that interview, it was like we had known each other our entire lives. After our interview concluded, the producer gave me Adam's number, and I reached out to him. Since then, I have invited him, along with his family, to my family's place out in Texas and even introduced him at a recent event in New Jersey (you're welcome, redneck cupid!). I say that jokingly because he doesn't look like someone who writes books; he looks like someone who should be a bouncer in a honky-tonk somewhere, though he's written several books on marriage and relationships for sheepdogs. We are proud to have Adam as a part of our *Team Never Quit* lineup of speakers.

Adam's writing and his speaking resonate with many because he is relatable. His story is powerful and a reminder that every American—including the blue-collar crowd, the working class, the backbone of our country—can overcome and live extraordinary lives of victory. I recognize warriors and the warrior spirit. That spirit is within every American, but too often, we get buried under the weight of life's burdens, and we get caught up in our heads. We let those thoughts begin to dictate our path and our lives.

If you adopt the Unconquered Code Adam has created here, you will find that you truly can live unconquered. You will realize just how possible it is for you to live above defeat and live victoriously, no matter what.

We are living in challenging times, but that's what Americans do. That's who we are. We don't back down in the face of adversity, and we don't back down when we have to face our pain. *Unconquered: 10 Principles to Overcome Adversity and Live above Defeat* will give you the courage to face your pain. So I think it is only appropriate that a Texan write the foreword and that the last story in the book is about a Texan who "ate shotgun shells for breakfast" and survived. Listen, our mission at *Team Never Quit* is to inspire people to stay in the fight, to remind them they are never out of the fight. Adam's mission is to remind you that you are never defeated as long as you stay in the fight.

If you know anything about most military service members (especially team guys) or other first responders, you know we aren't known for being "religious." But we do have faith, and we do hold that dear to our hearts. Adam will guide you on a path to revealing the mindset and spirit of a warrior and becoming someone who understands the importance of faith in a life unconquered.

I want to challenge you to read every word, adopt the Unconquered Code as part of your life, and practice the powerful principles Adam has provided in the following pages. If you do, you will not only come out stronger, but you will also learn what it means to *fight like hell* and live unconquered.

Never quit!

Marcus Luttrell
US Navy SEAL, Retired
Author of *Lone Survivor*
Host of the *Team Never Quit* podcast

## INTRODUCTION

# DON'T UNDERESTIMATE THE BATTLE

*"Which of you, desiring to build a tower,
does not first sit down and count the cost,
whether he has enough to complete it?"*

LUKE 14:28 ESV

Nearly three years after the attacks on Pearl Harbor, American victories in the Southwest and Central Pacific took the fight within close proximity of Japan in the Battle of Peleliu, which was codenamed Operation Stalemate. American bombers were within striking distance of the Japanese main islands from bases secured during a campaign known as the Mariana Islands campaign from June to August 1944. According to Major General William Rupertus, the commander of the First Marine Division, the battle was only supposed to last four days; however, the campaign to occupy the airstrip on Peleliu lasted nearly three months.

The United States emerged victoriously, but it came at a high cost. According to the Marine Corps University website, there were over six thousand casualties.[1] This island was crucial for the United States to take because of its proximity between the United States and Japan, and it ended up being one of the bloodiest battles in World War II. Since 2009, civilians and military members have discovered over thirty-two thousand munitions on Peleliu.[2] While the government has attempted to discharge these bombs to make the island safer, undetonated explosives remain, and now, many decades after this Pacific paradise was a war zone, tourists must adhere to warning signs and designated walkways because of the number of undetonated explosives.

When I think about the stories from the Battle of Peleliu, I'm reminded of how our past can affect every aspect of our lives. And in its allegorical form, it's an accurate representation of the way many feel defeated by past life experiences. Our past has the potential to be devastating to our present and future and can shape our perspective on life. We've all been like that Pacific island, a place where American forces fought heavy battles, and all that we recall are the charred remains and undetonated bombs, waiting for the moment they detonate and take out innocent relationships and sabotage good opportunities.

I don't know what you've battled or what caused you the most pain in life, but I know you're not alone in the fight. It's not my intention to come across as shortsighted here nor as insensitive, but the reality is that many of us have endured abuse, tragedy, and deep soul pain. It could have resulted from your job in service to your country and the things you have witnessed or had to do in the course of your duty. Or it could have come at the hands of a family member, friend, or neighbor in the form of sexual abuse or physical abuse as a child. But as American military leaders and first responders do after any training or operation, we should look at our lives and determine what lessons we can learn from the pain we've experienced.

Through the lessons my experiences have taught me, one thing I've taken away is the opportunity to learn from the pain. I have learned how to become a better version of myself, a stronger, more resilient version. Experiences teach us to expect pain, to endure, to embrace trials and suffering—not because we're strange but because we know there will be some good to come from it all. The addiction to comfort is killing our ability to reach our maximum potential. The addiction to ease and comfort creates weak societies.

We're a different generation than the breed of warriors who fought for our nation in World War II. When I think about the men who fought for America then, I think about a portion of Eugene Sledge's memoir entitled *With the Old Breed: At Peleliu and Okinawa*. In this acclaimed first-person account of the Battle of Peleliu, Sledge writes,

> It was hard to sleep that night [before the invasion]. I thought of home, my parents, my friends—and whether I would do my duty, be wounded and disabled, or be killed. I concluded that it was impossible for me to be killed, because God loved me. Then I told myself that God loved us all and that many would die or be ruined physically or mentally or both by the next morning and in the days following. My heart pounded, and I broke out in a cold sweat. Finally, I called myself a…coward and eventually fell asleep saying the Lord's Prayer to myself."[3]

Mr. Sledge provides an incredible perspective of someone facing what we could easily describe as a nightmare *if* we could fathom what he saw the next day and felt that night. Imagine knowing you were walking into a death trap tomorrow, and you still went. You trusted in God, and through him, you found your strength, your peace, and your blessed assurance. What assurance—that neither death nor life can separate us from the love of God! When we are in the throes of sorrow, his love may seem to be an eternity away, but that assurance and his promises are comforting and give us strength for the fight.

## Identify the Undetonated Explosives in Your Life

As you read this, the memories of life's battles may still be freshly lingering in your mind. The embers may still be red-hot from the fires that roared through your life. Right now, you may be experiencing soul-wrenching pain; it feels like your throat is being squeezed, and you can't breathe. Anxiety is a real thing. Panic attacks. I get it. You're still in the fight.

During my training phase in the police academy, we were taught how to handle a number of different potential dangers we might face on duty. Our instructors would bring up things like high-risk traffic stops, felony warrants, high-speed pursuits, foot pursuits, shoot-outs, and ground fighting. The reality is that you can spend your entire life training and preparing, and the only battle you get into is the one you didn't train to fight. There are going to be situations in which you are victorious only because of God. Otherwise, they are no-win situations.

I want to point out some clear strategies the enemy will use, some areas where our armor may have a vulnerability, how we can best prepare for what lies ahead, and how to best overcome what is behind us. It's important to identify the areas where the enemy may attack you before the campaign against you is advanced. Think about each of these areas and see if any apply to you.

1. **Ignoring the Pain:** Do you pretend it didn't happen? Ignoring the pain leads to a chain reaction of additional battles that you could avoid. Ignoring is not the answer, but addressing these wounds will lead to healing.

2. **Refusing to Surrender:** Do you try to control others or manipulate circumstances? When you try to heal through your own power, you're not surrendering as God intends. There's no such thing as controlling your surrender to God. It must be 100 percent, open hands, open hearts. We cannot control others, nor can we orchestrate or manipulate the circumstances of life in our favor. Relinquish control to the one who created life itself, be committed to taking the actions you are responsible for taking to find healing and freedom, and don't worry about what others do or say.

3. **Living in the Past:** If you are still celebrating a victory from ten years ago but not facing the battles that left you wounded, you have been deceived. There's a difference between living in the past and learning from it. Living in it keeps you from growing, maturing, and advancing. Learning from it makes you a mature, strong, and capable warrior who will overcome any battle that comes your way.

4. **Refusing to Forgive:** Maybe it makes you feel like you still retain some degree of wholeness, but it is not helping you at all. It's a lie from the enemy and one of the most sensitive of undetonated bombs in your life. Forgiving the offender sets you free.

5. **Emotions Gone Wild:** It may feel like you're the only one who has an emotional roller-coaster ride in life, but we need only look to the Old Testament to see how common this really is. David was an emotional wreck in the book of Psalms. But we must take captive our thoughts and emotions and align them with the truth of God's Word.

6. **Doing Things Your Way:** This makes for good song lyrics but not a good life. Being in total control of everything is exhausting and overrated.

7. **Toxic Relationships:** There are some folks you need to distance yourself from. You know who they are, and unless there is abuse present, I am not referring to your marriage.

8. **The Lost Wanderer:** All your time and energy are expended fighting to find your way. You lack direction, aren't clear on your purpose, and even wonder if it is all worth it. Pain can cause you to lose focus of your true north and divine purpose and throw you into a pit of confusion.

9. **The Know-It-All:** Your brain is stale, your heart is hard, and you've grown complacent. You're a statistic waiting to happen in every area of your life. It's time to get back to the warrior you were before the pain and before the pressure of life had an impact on you.

10. **You Quit Before You Start:** Quitting, like winning, begins in the mind; every time life gets hard, you want to quit. That changes here and now. Remove *quit* from your vocabulary and prepare to live on a different level of winning.

Those are ten notes I wrote to myself over the past several years as I navigated my own deep soul pain. I tried to carry it all on my own strength and abilities, and it almost killed me. The good news? You don't have to carry the burden of pain or past sin or the memories of traumatic experiences. We have a compassionate God, one who not only forgives us for those things when we trust Jesus with our lives but who also forgets that we ever did anything wrong. Throughout God's Word, we are reminded that, while he knows our pains, he keeps no record of the sins we give to him. Every aspect of our lives suffers when we allow the enemy to deceive us into believing we are too far gone, convince us that we are broken beyond repair, or cause us to be afraid of seeking help. The past has prepared us for the present—there are no accidents. We can either grow from it, learn from it, or wallow in it.

Fear is one battle we must all face. We must choose whether we will let fear lead us or whether we walk in faith. Those two things, fear and faith, cannot cohabitate in our lives. We must choose which one will be the primary influencer in our decisions, behaviors, thoughts, and words. We must also face the battle to forgive. God has forgiven us the moment we ask, but seeking the forgiveness of someone you have offended can be much more challenging.

The greater battle is whether you will forgive those who have deeply hurt you. If I were to ask you if those people who hurt you are worthy of forgiveness, you'd likely say no. It's hard for me to fathom why or how God can or would even consider forgiving some human beings for the atrocities they've committed, but then that's me judging. I can't decide who is forgiven or who isn't. Fear tells us that if we forgive someone who hurt us, then we are weak or setting ourselves up to be hurt again. I didn't feel like the people who hurt me deserved to be forgiven, and then I remembered that when I least deserve forgiveness, God still forgives me.

Many of our underlying issues are unaddressed wounds from past traumatic experiences. To find healing, it is required that we lay these wounds down. It begins here, remodeling our minds with a better way of thinking. I'm not a victim. I am more than a conqueror. Don't bottle it up as I did for over two decades. It bears no good fruit, only burdens and more pain.

During a battle, it's not uncommon to feel God has forsaken you; you are not alone! In Psalm 22:1 2 (NIV), David expressed feelings of anguish and abandonment, echoing what Jesus said on the cross:

> My God, my God, why have you forsaken me?
> Why are you so far from saving me,
> so far from my cries of anguish?
> My God, I cry out by day, but you do not answer,
> by night, but I find no rest.

If David, and Jesus, felt abandoned by God in the most painful places of their lives, I think it's okay if we acknowledge when we feel that way too. While this is not a book on trauma or pain specifically, it is written with the understanding that many have had life-changing traumatic experiences and still deal with the fallout from them to this day.

There's someone in your life you can reach out to, someone you can talk to, someone who is waiting for the opportunity to listen to you. Maybe you're healed, and it is you who is standing ready to reach out and help a brother or sister who is battling their own demons. We are all bearing scars from battles in this life, and none of us are unwounded, but we are all unconquered if we have surrendered our lives to Christ. Do not allow Satan to lure you into isolation because of your challenges. Fear will ruin your life. It can and will destroy you, and it is very seductive. Fear is empowered and given more authority in isolation.

## Matters of the Mind

What do you think of when you see the Disney franchise or the name Walt Disney? What about Benjamin Franklin? Let's add Vincent van Gogh, Stephen King, and Albert Einstein to the list. All the names listed above are people who have been incredibly successful, and we see the fruit of their labor to this day. But we often do not see the incredible adversity they endured and overcame to achieve greatness. Like Disney, Franklin, Van Gogh, King, or Einstein, under the pinnacle of success is a massive mountain of rejection, failure, disappointment, and pain. There are no "overnight" success stories. There is, however, a large population of people who have trained, attempted their feat, and lost. Their next step was to repeat steps one through three until they got it right.

It is my belief that we can learn something from everyone and from every circumstance, good or bad. Pleasurable or painful. Experiences that give us great joy or terrible sorrow. Mental defeat, sometimes abbreviated as MD, refers to the cognitive quit in your mind resulting from chronic pain or post-traumatic stress disorder (some refer to it as PTSD). If our minds quit, our bodies follow. And maybe you once had a dream, and you watched that dream die. Maybe you were on a journey to get fit and healthy, but you were injured and have regressed. Maybe your business venture failed, or maybe you've relapsed back into the grip of addiction. That's where we truly quit: in our minds.

We must train our minds to abandon the desire to quit, the need for easy or comfortable living. If our minds can overcome the desire to quit and push us further than we've ever been, our bodies will follow. But if our spirit is wounded, our minds and bodies have a significantly more challenging battle. Each of the individuals listed in the examples above overcame the desire to quit when they faced adversity.

Let's look deeper into their lives, starting with Walt Disney. He was fired from his first job because he was not "creative or imaginative" enough. Looking back, I think we can all agree that the person who fired him completely failed. Or did they? Was Walt Disney not creative or imaginative enough at the time? Perhaps those traits only developed and matured as he persisted and before launching the largest entertainment company in modern history.

What about Benjamin Franklin? At ten years of age, his parents could no longer afford to send him to school.

But he did not let that stop him from obtaining an excellent education. Instead of quitting, Franklin read books and educated himself, ultimately leading to the invention of lightning rods, bifocals, and other devices, not to mention his invaluable contributions as a writer, statesman, and diplomat.

During his lifetime, Vincent van Gogh sold one painting out of his nine hundred pieces of art. Now, long after his death, he remains one of the most influential figures of the Western arts.

One of my personal favorites is the story of Stephen King. Now, I am no fan of horror and gore, but the mind of Stephen King and his mastery of the craft of writing has made me a fan of his. King, one of the most successful writers of our time, had his first book rejected by over thirty publishers. He literally threw the book in the trash until his wife discovered it and encouraged him to finish it. He has since sold over 350 million copies of his books.

Albert Einstein didn't speak for the first three years of his life, and many of his teachers assumed he was just lazy because of his focus on abstract concepts. Ultimately, he would grow up and develop the theory of relativity, the quantum theory of light, and other important theories of matter and energy.

There have been a number of research studies conducted on the potential of the human mind, and some have inaccurately stated that we only use 10 percent of our brains, leaving 90 percent of our brainpower untapped. While this makes for good entertainment and the basis for many motivational theories, it's not totally accurate. What remains accurate is hard work. Give 100 percent effort 100 percent of the time and do it for the right reasons, with the right heart, the right way, all the time. Those United States Marines who took Peleliu didn't quit. Nor did the first responders who were at Ground Zero on September 11, 2001. Nobody remembers a quitter, and nobody remembers what you almost accomplished. We are limitless in our potential when we depend on the power of God to be our source of strength, the foundation of our endurance, and the light that leads us down the path of victory.

If you quit when it gets tough, you forfeit all the hard work, all the pain, the sacrifice, and the potential. If it's worth suffering for, it's worth enduring, and walking away from the battle to overcome adversity simply isn't an option. There are no great victories without great adversity, and our legacies are either going to be that we quit when things were overwhelming, when we were outnumbered and outmanned, or we will be remembered as being tenacious, relentless, and enduring. It's something we must decide in our minds, in our hearts, that we will absolutely do.

## The Unconquered Code

As you read this, I am sure it brings to the forefront of your mind some massive failure in your life, a point when you backed down, moved on, and left that mountain unconquered. Our human instinct is to do whatever is necessary to eliminate and escape the pain as fast as possible when too often there is a lesson to learn, a pinnacle to reach, and a gift to discover. I used to be a quitter, so I know the deep regret that comes with quitting when things get hard.

Throughout my life, I have always tried to figure out how things work, whether it was toy cars as a child or actual vehicles, firearms, computers, websites, or human behavior as an adult. In trying to figure out what lessons I can learn from my failures and pain, I have discovered something about myself and others. I am a husband to Amber, father to our three children, redeemed by God's love, but most of all, and because of God, I am unconquered. The pain in my life does not negatively define me, but I have tried to allow my experiences to shape me into a better person. Something else I have noticed is that there are some common principles of resilient people. Throughout this book, you will read some true stories, stories of people I know, people I have met, people from whom I have learned great lessons.

As I was preparing to write this book, I looked over my life and the lives of many people I have had the honor of meeting and learning about, and I discovered a few key principles. I call this the Unconquered Code:

1. Acknowledge the pain. Ignoring it doesn't make it disappear. Seek the heavenly healer.

2. Recognize you are in control of yourself and that you are in control of no one else.

3. Live in the present, hope for the future, and learn from the past.

4. Discover freedom in forgiveness. It's not for the offender; it's for you.

5. Take captive your emotions to align them with the truth of God's Word.

6. Experience true power through daily surrender to Christ.

7. Cherish your healthy relationships and distance yourself from toxic relationships.

8. Seek to know your divine and unique purpose in life and the direction God is leading you to take.

9. Accept responsibility for creating healthy daily habits in your life.

10. Resolve at this moment that no pain, no sin, no mistake, nothing in this world will defeat you. Your declaration today becomes *I am unconquered. In Christ I live; in Christ I die. I live unconquered; I die unconquered.*

Adopt this new code and put it into practice in your own life. I have taken the lessons learned through the most painful experiences and seen how these principles have worked for me. It's not always easy, and that's okay. Today, things may seem overwhelming. Your reason may be different from mine, but the mindset and approach to overcoming the past remain the same. Use these moments to discover who you are and who God created you to be.

Your past, your pain, or the events of your life do not define you. You are not a victim. God's Word defines you as more than a conqueror (see Romans 8:37). Knowing this empowers you to live up to the potential in your life and what the possibilities are for you when you open your hands and let God take the unaddressed pain from you. Our life experiences shape us, and we have a choice for how we can respond to painful circumstances. The freedom to choose is one beauty of this life. And the choice to heal, grow, and live unconquered, no matter how difficult, is still a viable option for every person.

As you begin this journey to living unconquered, I intend to expose the lies of hell, the strategies the enemy will use against you, and the many hazards that will pop up along the way. The power of God is what sets us free; it's what will set individuals free from their personal prisons of the past and set them on a path to healing and freedom in Christ.

This story isn't about a victim. This is a story of an overcomer, a victor, someone set free to overcome the effects of trauma. But my story isn't the only one of its kind. If you've experienced traumatic events in your life and have carried the burden of those memories alone, this story is yours. This victory flag is for everyone who has ever shed tears as they dealt with deep soul pains and for those who are still fighting.

So we begin. We begin the journey down a new path to develop new habits, discover untapped strength, and see the reality of what it means to live unconquered. Too often, our faith ends when we repeat a short prayer during a church service and call that being saved or born again. Jesus didn't stay on the cross, but too often our perspective of salvation ends there. He was raised from a borrowed tomb, and before he ascended to heaven, he promised us the source of true power and victory, the Comforter, the Holy Spirit. It is my prayer that, as you navigate these next few chapters, you will accept the challenges you will face and face them with vigor and enthusiasm. If you will resolve to live above defeat in faith, through Christ, your life will never be the same. You will come to realize that every time you didn't feel good enough or every time you felt defeated, it was an attack on your destiny; it was a lie.

This becomes our battle cry. No matter how deep the pain, in Christ, I am unconquered. My victory is in him.

## The Unconquered Challenge

Throughout the coming chapters, I will present strategic actions you can take as an individual to develop an unconquered mindset. One of the things that I have used to help me overcome various challenges is journaling along with daily devotion time. But for the next thirty days, I want to challenge you to join me in writing down your actions for each chapter. Each chapter will provide you with a Battle Action Step with three questions. Here is your challenge:

1.  Purchase a journal and begin writing daily as you navigate through this journey.

2.  Set aside time each day to read through this book and process the discussion questions and prompts.

3.  Write down your responses to the questions and the action you take relating to the Battle Action Step.

4. Print off the Unconquered Code from the website www.UnconqueredBook.com and frame it. Remember it and refer to it as needed. Make it a way of life.

5. Ask a few of your closest friends or family members to join you on this journey.

6. Most importantly, ask God to guide you through this journey, to give you the courage, the willpower, and the stamina to see it through.

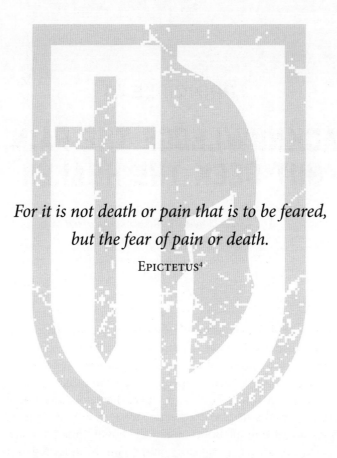

*For it is not death or pain that is to be feared,*
*but the fear of pain or death.*

Epictetus[4]

# ACKNOWLEDGE THE PAIN, BUT SEEK THE HEALER

*The LORD is near to the brokenhearted
and saves the crushed in spirit.
Many are the afflictions of the righteous,
but the LORD delivers him out of them all.*

PSALM 34:18–19 ESV

To live undefeated, we must quit lying to ourselves about what causes us the most pain in our lives. Peeling back what seemed to be layers of old wounds was painful for me. It requires courage, trust, and vulnerability to pursue healing, but it is worth it. Not all pain hurts the same, and not all trauma results in post-traumatic stress. Now, this is not a book about trauma, but trauma will be mentioned in places because it is part of my story, and so are healing, redemption, and hope. *Trauma*, as discussed in this book, is a type of deep soul hurt. The American Psychological Association defines *trauma* as "an emotional response to a terrible event like an accident, rape or natural disaster."[5] In the wake of a terrible event, it is not uncommon to become wounded in ways others cannot see with their eyes. You see, there's no way to plaster the wounds of trauma on billboards, television commercials, or social media. You can't see it, but if you're the one who is experiencing it, you know how real it is.

Maybe you can relate to me here: I have a propensity to hide my wounds, whether because of pride, shame, or maybe fear. It's something that goes back to my childhood. I remember one instance as a little boy when I was playing in an area where I was told not to be, near a guy wire, the support that runs from the top of a power or utility pole to the ground at an angle, usually covered with a hard, yellow, plastic material. I fell onto it and severely cut my arm. Because I was afraid of punishment for being somewhere I was not supposed to be, I tried to treat the cut on my own, as a child. Eventually, it became infected, and the wound required stitches. In hindsight, I should have taken whatever consequences resulted from my disobedience and received treatment sooner for my arm. While that cut hurt and the physical punishment for being somewhere I wasn't supposed to be would have hurt, it didn't affect my emotions. I didn't mourn the cut, and I didn't have a negative emotional response to it. While my physical body experienced a terrible cut, my soul was not wounded. Soul wounds are more profound, a different kind of pain, and they don't always occur due to physical injury.

I never engaged in an officer-involved shooting as a law enforcement officer. And I've never been in a gunfight. But, like many others, I *have* been wounded; you just can't see it. The evil and destruction of the human body—often glamorized by films, video games, and television—aren't healthy for human beings to witness so often. And no matter what you may think, no one should ever have to see some of the things military personnel and first responders see daily. For me, I accepted the deep-seated wounds in my soul as a life sentence, and for many years, I lived with it and neglected the path to healing. I'm not sure who taught me to carry it on my own, but that is what I tried to do.

## I'll Never Forgive Them

When I write about forgiveness, it's from personal experience. Forgiveness didn't come easy for me, and there were a number of times when I said, "I will never forgive them." I know what it is to harbor incredible hatred and resentment and how it feels to harbor a grudge. I know how it feels to think there's no way I could *ever forgive* or live without the burdens of my past. So, I will bare my soul with you in the following pages. Some areas will be intense. And if you have experienced similar wounds as I describe, my story may garner some nasty thoughts and emotions. So, stay with me, and let's take these steps together with our healer.

A common saying, often attributed to Mark Twain, advises, "Eat a live frog first thing in the morning, and nothing worse will happen to you the rest of the day." What he implied was that you should do the most difficult things first, that which you most dread, and the rest will come easier. Now, I'm not one to eat live frogs, but I will eat a figurative frog here. Sharing these things in front of audiences for the past decade has made me stronger, served as a method of healing, and touched thousands of lives. But writing about it, well, that's a much larger frog.

But before the frog entrée, a sidenote. I will not mention the names of the individuals who abused me, condoned it, or excused it, and it is not because I am afraid of them. It's because I don't believe they should receive any spotlight, lest they make themselves out to be some type of martyr or hero. I hold the same belief when an evil person takes a firearm and commits murder in a school, business, or church; I don't believe we should ever mention their names. It empowers them, emboldens them, and gives them a spotlight that they do not deserve. We should honor and remember the victims, not the offenders.

Over the past three decades, I've learned a great deal about trauma, pain, and how our minds and bodies respond to it all. Some of it I have learned through my experiences, and other parts I've learned from observing humanity. I believe we all have experienced pain so unspeakable that it still affects us. The effects can last a lifetime if we let them.

Since 2015, I've traveled the United States sharing my life story with audiences of first responders, military service members, and civilians. On each occasion, I've tried my best to be authentic and vulnerable with the pain in my life, although it isn't always easy. And throughout my travels and meeting new people, I've met some incredible friends who have experienced the worst types of pain. I think about people like Houston Gass, a Texas law enforcement officer who was shot in the face by a felon; Marcus Luttrell, a retired US Navy SEAL who was the lone survivor of a Taliban ambush; and my mother-in-law, Angie Adams, who lost one of her young sons to leukemia.

As I think about them and so many others, I am inspired. They have, in some way, encouraged me, challenged me, and sharpened me. Yet there's something each person I've met who experienced devastating loss or incredible pain has in common: they are resilient. They didn't give up or back down on the worst days of their lives. I see them as unconquered, and I am thankful for each of them.

Whether it is through public speaking or writing books, my mission is to let people know there is a better way of living. Your past does not define you; neither does the pain you've experienced or the mistakes you made. I want others to experience the love and peace that has changed my life.

In January 2021, I traveled to a small town in Minnesota to speak to a group of law enforcement officers. While preparing, I researched many issues they were facing and titled the talk "Live Unconquered." On the flight back home, something clicked in my brain. As I sat aboard the aircraft somewhere around thirty-seven thousand feet in the air, it hit me. *That's it! That's it, Adam*, I said to myself. *We are unconquered!* We've faced many battles, and we bear many scars, wounds, and terrible memories, but we are still in the fight. As long as you're still battling, you aren't defeated.

I finished speaking to a group of first responders, about 150 or so, and I was standing by the table where I was signing books when one man walked up to me, lifted his shirt, revealing scars, and said, "You think I am unconquered? A bullet can conquer anyone if it hits them in the right place. I can't do what I love anymore because of my injuries. So please tell me, how can I possibly be unconquered? Because, to be honest with you, I'm feeling defeated and deflated right now."

He was right. A bullet, a train, a rocket, a meteor, a knife, a freak accident can end our careers, change our lives, or even end our lives. But living unconquered isn't just about this life; it's a way of life, *the Way*. It's a mindset and often opposite of anything this world teaches us to do. My life changed when I surrendered to Jesus and gave him the burdens I had carried for so long.

## I Can't Do This Anymore

For nearly two decades, I carried a burden that nearly destroyed me. I'm not a doctor, therapist, counselor, or expert of any kind, but I would think maybe some of my childhood burdens have something to do with my development through childhood, teenage years, and even into adulthood. Perhaps it was one of the reasons I had problems with reading comprehension, among other issues. Don't misinterpret what I am saying here; I accept full responsibility for every mistake, every sin, every wrong decision I've made, but there's some effect on us when traumatic things happen at such a young age.

I often open my talks by sharing something humorous to break the ice and then dive right into the hard stuff, you know, like eating the frog type of thing. I don't have any humor at this point in the book, so here goes the hard stuff: I was raped and sodomized when I was five. That's also when I first saw pornography.

It was an older man, unrelated to my family, who took me into a room, which I just so happen to remember was blue, where he made me sit in front of a TV and watch some of the filthiest things you *don't* want to imagine. I don't remember all of what I saw, but some scenes remained seared in my brain for decades. It wasn't long before the man began "role-playing" with me based on the scenes he made me watch beforehand. He forced me to do things I wouldn't feel comfortable documenting in a book. What followed this series of events was a childhood of pain, confusion, shame, and guilt. I remember in the following years being taken to a doctor because I couldn't control my bowel movements and a speech therapist because I developed a speech impediment. Nobody understood why, but looking back, I understand it may have had something to do with my development as a child through those reprehensible events.

According to society, we're not supposed to talk about this sort of stuff. I get that; it's taboo to mention it, especially for men. Others may think it makes me look weak, and for some, well, it makes them uncomfortable. Please hear me out on this. If we don't expose this sort of thing, we will never deal with it in our lives or in our world. If we keep evil shrouded in darkness and secrecy, it remains powerful. When we expose it to the light, it gives others the courage to face their experiences as well.

I am here to flip on the light switch in your life through meeting Jesus. The power of God is real. I am a living testament to his power and just how real he is. I'm not talking about a feel-good moment in a special church service, although those are meaningful to me. I am talking about a real encounter with the living God. Expose your pain to him.

You see, I still remember that room vividly. I remember the smell of the room, the blue walls, and the moments leading up to the point of pain. I remember what that man did to me and what he made me do as a little boy. The difference is that now it doesn't have any impact on me. I can talk about it and now write about it without being tossed into an endless loop of negative thoughts and emotions. But that hasn't always been the case.

As a teenager and almost ten years after the blue room pain, I was often left in the care of a married woman who was a leader in a local church. We talked like we were both the same age, but she was twice my age and married with children. The first night I was left in her care, she made alcoholic drinks for me although I was not even old enough to drive. Then we had sex. As I look back, it seemed to be all orchestrated perfectly. But by whom? I'm not sure, but the enemy was certainly involved.

This went on for about a year as she—and the people around her who knew what was going on—groomed me to believe it was a God-ordained relationship. "God sent you to help me through a difficult time in my life, and you are part of my healing. I love you," she said. It only ended when I told my father that I thought something wasn't right.

While some in our society will think, "Man, you're lucky," I will say to you now, unequivocally, I wish it had never happened. I wish someone would have told me, "I don't care what she or anyone else says; it's not God's will, and God didn't set this up!" Because that's what she told me, that it was "God's will" for it to happen. I lost my virginity to a married woman as a drunk teenager. My perspective of relationships, church, and God was flawed. Had I not been an isolated teenager and had I known more about manipulation and deception, especially from people I was supposed to be able to trust, maybe I would have known it wasn't God's will and that I was being fed a line of lies. Deception, manipulation, and pain were the highlights of my childhood. My naivety has played a role in protecting me many times as an adult, but as a child, it cost me.

## Before We Bleed Out

My wife and I have been married for over twenty years. We were married at the age of eighteen, and while I disclosed to her what had happened to me at fifteen years old and as a five-year-old boy, neither of us knew the full extent of how it affected me. I lacked the emotional ability and maturity to navigate these issues, and as a new husband, I fell short on many occasions because of it. All I knew to do was to run from trouble to hide the pain. It was an expensive and confusing game of hide-and-seek.

Trauma of any type can affect our ability to trust, have healthy relationships, and be productive members of society. However, the greatest threat trauma can have on our well-being isn't the physical symptoms; it's the unseen consequences. It's the development of depression as adults, severe anxiety disorders, and worst of all, the wedge of division created between God and us.

I've often wondered what my childhood would have looked like had I not been lured into the blue room. Who would I have become without those experiences? Would I have been a better husband for Amber when we first married? The number of tears I have shed because of physical pains is vastly outnumbered by the number of tears shed because of soul pain resulting from the blue room and as a teenager. But our heavenly Father knows each tear we shed, and he knows every pain we have experienced. He is near to the brokenhearted.

## The Monster and the Serpent

I think our lives before traumatic events are similar to the garden of Eden before the fall of man. The garden of Eden was perfect the way God created it, untarnished, with no sin, and for every need, there was provision. Enter the serpent, who deceived Eve, which led to the fall of humanity. The monster in the blue room and the serpent in the garden of Eden aren't much different. Trauma in our lives does the same thing the serpent did in the garden of Eden; it disturbs the peace we possess. It robs us of peace, joy, and being whole and well. It steals our innocence and shatters our souls. The breaking place for you may be much different from the breaking place in my life. Chances are that the details of the sources of our pain are not similar at all. But there is one thing that *is* the same: the source of healing.

The Bible calls Satan "the prince of the power of the air" (Ephesians 2:2 ESV). He is the great deceiver and the Father of Lies, and his sole mission is to kill, steal, and destroy (see John 10:10). Yes, he uses trauma to accomplish his mission. But *your* pain isn't the end of your story; it's up to you. You decide whether you pursue healing from trauma or if you choose to remain where you are.

In the Gospel of John, Jesus said, "I have told you these things, so that in me you may have peace. In this world you will have trouble. But take heart! I have overcome the world" (16:33 NIV). From Genesis to Revelation, we read story after story of conflict, terrible betrayal, pain, sin, and the depravity and brokenness of humanity. Satan isn't victorious, and brokenness isn't the end. Jesus came so we could overcome the troubles of this world. He is the hope for the hopeless, healing for the wounded, and peace for the troubled and weary souls.

## From Broken to Beloved

If we're not careful, we can become desensitized to the pain in our lives because we talk about it so much, and discussing past pain makes it sound like a walk in the park. But it's not; I get it. It's one thing to talk about the pain of the past. It's another to navigate through the storms of life while you try to apply biblical principles in a mess. You see, it's easy to quit. But running from what has haunted us, some of us for decades, just means we have a greater chance of failure, defeat, and more layers of pain.

In our society, we are accustomed to discarding broken things. When was the last time you tried to repurpose a shattered dinner plate or fine glassware? Never! We are more apt to repair the broken screens on our smartphones than we are to restore the wounds of our souls! After the blue room and especially as a teenager, I felt like my life was completely ruined. My ability to trust or even develop relationships was severely affected. Today, as you read this, you may feel the same way. And, if we're being completely honest with ourselves, we would rather throw away our marriages, and even our own lives, when things get rough.

Psalm 34:18 speaks to the brokenhearted ones: "The LORD is close to the brokenhearted and saves those who are crushed in spirit" (NIV). God is close to those who are afflicted, those who have had an emotional response to traumatic events. He is near. Our job is to believe in him and allow him the place in our hearts to do the work on what hurts most.

I'm not sure what it is about the breaking place that causes us to seek God more fervently, but it is not uncommon for our prayers to increase in frequency when the pain level is notched up a few spots. There's no other person who can comfort you, heal you, and ease your pain like Jesus. He's not a fictional character from a child's story. He's more than the felt storyboard character you saw in Sunday school, and he's more than the blue-eyed, blond-haired figure you saw in portraits and giant family Bibles. He is a warrior-healer. He calls us his *own*. Yes, even at our point of pain, no matter how deep the trauma hurts our souls, he sees us as precious, valuable, and worth redeeming.

He is close to you, me, and all others who have been brokenhearted and crushed in spirit. In this life, we will face challenges, pain, and, as Jesus said it, "trouble." The enemy will try to get inside your head using the memories of your past experiences, and he will use negative emotions to create a wedge between you and God. Listen, the same voice that lured me into the blue room, the same voice that tells many they will never be healed or overcome the trauma of their past, originates in hell. It is a lie of the enemy. Because of sin, we are inherently rotten, evil, and vile, and the only way to be made whole is by redemption through Christ. In our brokenness, he calls us his beloved, his very own. There's nothing that compares to the love of Christ. No matter who surrounds us and no matter how bad the events in our lives, he is available if we cry out to him.

## In Unwelcomed Company

For the longest time, I thought I was the *only* boy to experience such abuse in life. And with that thought came a tremendous amount of shame, guilt, and feelings of complete filth. But I *wasn't* the only boy to be sexually abused, violated, and robbed of innocence. There are many. One in nine girls and one in fifty-three boys under the age of eighteen experience sexual abuse at the hands of an adult.[6] If you have been a victim of sexual abuse, you are not alone. No, that's not supposed to give you the perfect comfort you need to heal, but it is a necessary truth we must know. You are not alone in this battle. That's the fundamental truth we need. You're not alone, and the pain doesn't have to be the defining factor for your life.

The majority of offenders are men, but women are sexual abusers of children too.[7] To think of our society glamorizing sexual deviancy in any way, for any reason, should sound an alarm in the heart of every follower of Christ. We've been desensitized to these issues through movies, books, and headlines. We've relegated ourselves to being "okay" with a moment when we express disgust, but we do nothing further about it.

But sexual deviancy isn't the only thing we've become desensitized to as a society. We have become incredibly tolerant of terrible violence, murder, and bloodshed. We devour movies, video games, and books depicting such evil. It's an *expected* and *accepted* behavior in our nation. Maybe that's why we don't talk about our monsters. And maybe that's why, according to the National Council for Mental Wellbeing, 70 percent of adults in the US have experienced some type of traumatic event at least once in their lives.[8] That's 223.4 million people, or roughly two-thirds of the American population.

Think about this: based on those statistics, two out of every three people you know have experienced a traumatic event at least once in their lives. Not every person who experiences a traumatic event will experience post-traumatic stress because we all respond differently to pain. But many will! We must teach children to talk about pain and trauma and tell us if sexual offenses happen to them. But as critical as it is to teach children to talk about these issues, we, as adults, must find the courage to talk about our pain, our wounds, and our breaking place. We've been taught to keep our mouth shut, to suffer in silence, and that is not the way.

Maybe you are one of the one out of three who has never experienced a traumatic event, and maybe you are one of the fifty-two of fifty-three boys or eight of the nine girls who has never been sexually abused. Or, perhaps you have, and it didn't affect you like it did others. But, as the body of Christ, we should bear one another's burdens. When one is hurting, we should comfort them and lead them to lives restored by Jesus.

## Killing the Monster's Memory

I know there is a significant risk of being criticized and even humiliated for sharing my story. But this isn't the end of it. While sexual abuse traumatized me, I have been redeemed, set free, and made whole. Knowing millions of Americans have experienced similar abuse in their lives drives me to continue being courageous and sharing the testimony God has given me in overcoming these pains. Between the events of my childhood and teenage years, along with my career in law enforcement, my mission is to help others who have experienced trauma, not just sexual trauma but *any* trauma, to find the same freedom and healing.

As I have shared my story on stages across the United States, countless men and women have approached me, saying something to the effect of, "You gave me the courage to face my pain. You gave me the courage to begin truly healing." In one of my events a few years ago, I spoke to a large group of men in the church, sharing what I am sharing with you. At the end of the service, we had a time of corporate prayer at the altar. With tears streaming down his face, one man asked the pastor for a microphone. He stood in front of the crowd of men and said, "For over forty-five years, I have been a good husband to my wife and a good father to our kids, but my wife has never had the husband she will have after tonight, and our kids have never had the daddy they will have after tonight. Adam gave me the courage to forgive the monster from my childhood, and I have been given the power to be set free!"

If you're wondering, right now, why anyone would share such personal and horrible things from his life, that is why I share mine. And, no, I do not believe I am the one who heals. The source of every person's healing and redemption is Jesus alone. However, Scripture does say we overcome the enemy by the blood of the Lamb and the word of our testimony, so consider this to be my right hook to the left side of the enemy's jaw.

I am a father, a husband, and an utterly imperfect follower of Christ. But for more than twenty years, I was incredibly unstable in my career choices, relationships, and decision-making. Quitting came easy to me, but forgiving did not. I learned to hold grudges early, and I learned to hide pain before I was six. It wasn't until I was willing to surrender to Christ the nastiness in my heart and mind about the events from my childhood that I began healing. And there are millions of men and women today trying to live with these unhealed wounds in their souls. We live in difficult times, and this means we need men and women who give their pain to Christ and take the daily journey to discover healing and freedom available only through Christ. If you are hurting, I encourage you to seek him, devour his Word, and apply it.

I hope your story is different. I pray that I *am* the only one, but I know I am not. Maybe you're reading this, and you say, "Adam, I've never been sexually abused in any way. What about watching my friends die? What about losing a partner in the line of duty? What about being shot?" After any of these traumatic situations, healing is hard, but it is worth it, and the same God who heals those who have been sexually abused can heal any other wound to the soul caused by the evil of another human being or even natural disasters. These issues are complex, and they may require you to seek the counsel of a pastor, chaplain, or professional therapist.

The first step, however, is acknowledging the presence of pain in your life and then, through faith, taking that pain to our heavenly healer. Just like the enemy of our souls can use other people and events to drive us deeper into isolation from a relationship with God, God can use other people to bring you healing in your life. The first step to living unconquered is healing.

## Unconquered Code #1

Acknowledge the pain. Ignoring it doesn't make it disappear. Seek the heavenly healer.

## Battle Action Step

Think about one thing you can acknowledge that is hindering you from being made whole.

## Discussion

1. Are there certain memories that continue to cause you pain?

2. What can you do to acknowledge specific battles in your life?

3. What steps will you commit to taking today to begin pursuing our healer?

## Prayer

*Heavenly Father, I give you my pain. I give you the monsters of my past and the trauma that has imprisoned me from being the person you created me to be. Give me the courage and willpower to pursue you and find healing in the process. Amen.*

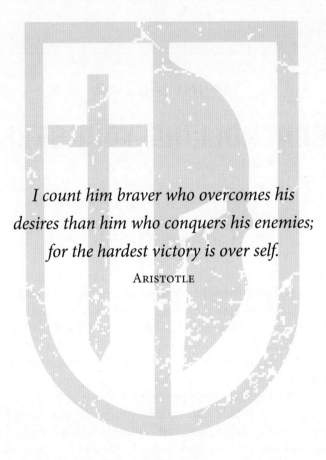

*I count him braver who overcomes his*
*desires than him who conquers his enemies;*
*for the hardest victory is over self.*

ARISTOTLE

## PRINCIPLE #2

# CONTROLLING YOURSELF

*This I call to mind, and therefore I have hope: The steadfast love of the LORD never ceases; his mercies never come to an end; they are new every morning; great is your faithfulness.*

LAMENTATIONS 3:21–23 ESV

There are people in this world who have chosen to allow the evil of hell itself to be their inspiration. All they know is hate. Whether they know the source of their hate is Satan really doesn't matter. Satan doesn't show up with a pitchfork and horns on his head; he shows up as the person who cuts you off in traffic, the person who raped you, the person who tried to kill you.

But just like those people who chose to be used for evil, there are people who are totally surrendered to the purpose God has for them and who allow him to use them for his glory. Now, I no longer wear a badge and duty belt full-time, and I no longer patrol the streets of my community, so there's not a lot I can do about the evil in my part of the world unless it comes to my doorstep or if I witness it in progress. What I can do is take care of myself and share the healing power of Jesus with the world, the truth of what his Word says about who we are.

We can't control the world or other people. If you're a law enforcement officer, you can arrest someone, but you can't decide their fate in court. They can walk away free even when you do everything by the book. You cannot change their heart or behavior. All you can do is control yourself. For my entire life, I have tried to control everything around me. I tried to control my relationships and the outcome of circumstances beyond my control, all while neglecting to deal with my own issues.

Society often teaches us that if we talk about stuff like this or if we seek help, then we're broken, but that's just a cop-out and a lie. I'd allowed some situations in my life (rejection, manipulation, pain) to cause me to have an issue with my own self-worth and value as a person. One day, Amber came to me and said, "I need you to do me a favor, honey." Normally that means there's some honey-do I've procrastinated finishing, so I immediately started thinking about projects or things I hadn't finished yet.

I responded, "Uh oh. What did I not get done? Name it, and I will get on it."

"It's nothing like that, babe. I need you to talk with someone, please. This whole deal with you not thinking you're good enough is wreaking havoc on our marriage and on you and your life in general. I see it, and I want you to get help with it, please." She wasn't pushy and didn't nag, but with a gentle and loving tone, she explained that she wanted to see me be made whole.

It's taken us a long time to see the effects a lifetime of pain have caused and how they were creating havoc in my life. I'm not sure if I was just exhausted from fighting or if my wife's suggestion was a sign that someone else cared about my struggles enough to mention it, but I didn't hesitate. I reached out to a friend of mine, someone I trust, a retired law enforcement officer, and asked who he would recommend. With tears in my eyes and a lump in my throat, I told him, "I don't know who to trust, so I will borrow yours. If you trust them, I will trust them. Will you recommend someone and do an introduction, please?"

So, in 2021, for the first time in my life, I sought the help of a therapist. Not just any therapist but one who specializes in trauma therapy and something called "eye movement desensitization and reprocessing," or EMDR for short. If you haven't heard of it before, it may sound like some wizardry when someone describes it, but it is absolutely legitimate, and I highly recommend it.

My first call with my therapist was like a breath of fresh air. It was like I had come up from being held underwater for thirty years. I can't help what other people did to me as a child or a teen or what I've experienced in my adult life, but I can control how I respond to it. And responding to pain the right way is an important pivot in the process of healing and restoration.

Making the decision to seek help from a reputable therapist did not come easy, but it was an absolute godsend. She took me in, maybe that same day; I don't clearly recall. What relief it was to have someone who could guide me through this process of healing not just from the pain but also the whole notion that I was defeated, finished, and waiting to die. I felt like I was a wasted life, nothing but pain, trouble, and mistakes. Then I realized the source of those thoughts: they originated from hell, from the same place every moment of pain in my life came from. I will never forget the first four sessions and the freedom I discovered through the help of my therapist.

To this day, I still talk with my therapists on occasion, and they still check in with me. But I've realized God has put so many talented and gifted individuals in my life who are professional therapists. I always joke that when I asked for a team to help me on this mission, God sent me about a half-dozen therapists, so it took a team to get me through all this mess. I laugh, and they look at me like I am crazy. It's a good time. I love the people in my life, though, and unlike before, I know I am not a burden. I know that because of Jesus, I am good enough. The truth of it all is that he came and died for us when we were a mess. He knew we would need it, so even when most of our friends and family would say we are a wreck, Jesus says we are good enough to die for, and to me, that's the standard.

We cannot measure our value as human beings by the opinions of other people, especially people who don't know the pain we've experienced, the places we've walked through in life, or the relationship we have with Jesus. I know this: I'm grateful for people who didn't give up on me when they had every right to. That is love. That is the best way to help someone through a battle—love them enough to walk with them through it all.

Since talking with my therapist, I've discovered my worth is not found in my gifts, what I can offer the world, or even in my story. My worth is in Jesus. I've also discovered I cannot make other people change, and all I can do is work on relinquishing control to God. It means until someone else is ready to get help, I can't force them to get help. All I can do is work on making sure I am where I need to be, doing the right things for the right reason and with the right heart.

### Inside the Pit

Navigating this life can feel a lot like when you get lost on a hike in the woods. You don't know where to turn or where to go. It can be an unsettling feeling, but we can learn something about this from the story of Joseph found in Genesis 37 in the Bible. Joseph was on a journey to locate his brothers as his father instructed him. The brothers were supposed to be in the field grazing the flock. While he was in the field looking for them, a man found him wandering and told Joseph his brothers had moved on to Dothan. Joseph's brothers hated him, and their animosity for Joseph was intense! His father, Jacob, had made Joseph a precious robe made of many colors. But when they met him in Dothan, Joseph's brothers ripped the robe from him and threw him into a pit.

Now, verse 24 tells us the pit they threw him into "was empty" and "there was no water in it" (ESV). He lacked what we lack when we navigate trauma on our own: other people who can relate to where we are and immediate provision for the needs we have at that moment. Joseph didn't stay in the pit long, and while we don't know precisely how long he was down there, we know that when Reuben, one of his brothers, returned to the pit, Joseph's other brothers had already removed him and sold him as a slave (see verse 29).

Maybe you can relate to Joseph's situation in a few ways. Maybe, like Joseph, you did the right things only to end up tossed aside and hurting. When we experience the hard places in this life, it can feel like we have been thrown into an empty pit with nobody to lean on and no real knowledge of how to escape it. It can feel like taking a hike in the woods and getting lost, not knowing how to find our way back to where we started. When we carry the effects of these events without seeking help, it is not uncommon to feel like we have become enslaved to those past events, like we now belong to the woods instead of on the path to healing and victory. When we choose to address these symptoms in our own ways, we enslave ourselves to a lifestyle of defeat. Sure, you can find some temporary reprieve from the pain, but deep down, those issues are fermenting and continuing to grow. It's like putting a Band-Aid on a fractured leg, completely useless and foolish!

For the longest time, I tried to address the issues from my childhood and experiences in law enforcement on my own, and for years, on occasion, it would feel like I couldn't breathe or even catch a breath. It was like I was being strangled. When the enemy can cut off our air supply, he controls our ability to fight. He will do everything he can to keep a wedge between us and a relationship with God.

If he can snuff out our reliance on the power of the Holy Spirit, he takes our spiritual breath, which brings me to an important point. In the New Testament, the word *Spirit*, when used in the context of "Holy Spirit," is *pneuma* in Greek, which was the language used to write the New Testament. *Pneuma* means "breath." If you feel like your spirit is breathless, it may be time to get back to relying on the power of the Holy Spirit and operating in the supernatural to find your joy again instead of being choked off from the power of God and the supply of our life.

The enemy will try to control our ability to continue in the battle by using a number of strategies to distract and divide us, and if we give in to that strategy, we eventually submit to whatever dominates us. I lived like this for over twenty years, and it is life-sucking, draining, and soul-crushing. As I travel across the United States talking to audiences, I have encountered many who have been enslaved to their past for decades. This is not a form of enslavement where the shackles are visible as steel cuffs and chains, but the symptoms are very clear.

Traumatic events don't have to be the end of you. They don't have to be the defining factor in your life, but they can be the place God uses to bring you closer to him. Think about this: Joseph's brothers threw him in a pit, and he survived. Daniel was thrown into the lions' den, left for dead, but God preserved him. Shadrach, Meshach, and Abednego were thrown into the fire, but there was another who protected them.

When we find ourselves being affected by a terrible event, it can seem overwhelming, but there was life before that event, and if we look to Christ, instead of the methods of our own might, we will find healing. If we continue to fight in our own power, the effects of our pain will be felt for years not only by ourselves but also by all whom we love and care about. It's a spiral out of control and deeper into pain, misery, and hopelessness.

The good news is that when we take responsibility for our own actions and realize we cannot control the actions of others, we take an important step toward living victoriously. There are some things we can do daily to help make this a reality, and it's not a worship of self-development. Rather, it is an acknowledgment of victory through total surrender to God. This isn't about living your best life. It's about living the life God meant for you to live: a life lived victoriously as more than a conqueror.

## Control before the Battle

In the previous chapter, I shared my personal experiences as a child, a teenager, and even my time in law enforcement. I don't want to rehash those things, but throughout that chapter, I told you how my emotional response to traumatic events affected my life in various ways. Now, I don't remember much before the first time I experienced a traumatic event in my life. Not because my memory is terrible but because I was very young. I do know trauma affects our memory to some degree because there are things I do not remember during my law enforcement career. Not specific details but blocks of time just gone. Thankfully, there's an abundance of paperwork that comes with that profession, so someone knows! If you ask me questions about police calls I responded to, I can answer them, but to recall them on my own, it's just blank. Trauma affects everyone differently, and sometimes, it causes us to have zero recollection of specific events. I don't know if that is just how pain affects us or if it is a way God heals us.

## Controlling Yourself

Maybe you have experienced the same memory issues, and the only thing you know is that the worst battles you've fought came against someone you loved and cared about, someone you thought loved you equally. After all, before being thrown into a pit and subsequently sold into slavery, Joseph was pasturing a flock with his brothers. Yes, the same brothers who hated him! It's not uncommon. When people we love cause us great pain, it makes it challenging to trust others to find healing. Not everyone is on a mission from hell to destroy you. God has his own operatives in this world, and they are good at what they do for him.

Our lives before the "worst day" were different. Do you remember? We saw the world differently if we can remember that far back. Now, not everyone develops what is known as post-traumatic stress disorder as a result of traumatic experiences. Many do but not everyone.

Think of trauma as a pit. It's a pit that, if we're not careful, becomes our new home. We find ourselves stuck, and in the process, we lose ourselves, our marriages, our families, our careers, and everything else about us. We lose our identity, and the pain becomes our new name. Whatever defined us *before* the traumatic event is now seemingly stripped away in the pit, but we don't *have* to be defined by those events. We will all respond differently to the events of this life and the various degrees of pain we will be exposed to. But our identity is not defined in the pain. You are still the strong, resilient, and powerful person you were before. There is hope for a better way of life, and this is not the end of you.

You may not remember anything before trauma became the biggest challenge in your life, but whether you remember or not, this is a new point to pivot. You are not defined by those events, and you are not defined by how you responded to them, either emotionally or mentally.

Remember this: trauma is not your master, your lord, or your god. There are different depths to the pit of pain, trauma, and even sin. If you're now free from this pit in your own life, consider how you can support friends and family who may be experiencing these issues. You can now help them find proper help to heal. You can't help others out of the shackles of pain if you're still wearing your own chains. Let's identify these issues and get on the path of living unconquered. Let's get out of the woods of trauma and a defeated mindset so we can fight for each other.

## Identifying Trauma Pits

Not all pits are the same, and not everyone is looking to throw you into one. Some folks are affected by a single event, while others are affected by repeated and prolonged exposure to traumatic events, and there are some who experience multiple traumatic events. We know there are essentially three different types of trauma pits:

- **Acute Trauma:** This results from a single stressful or dangerous event.
- **Chronic Trauma:** This results from repeated and prolonged exposure to highly stressful events. Examples include cases of child abuse, bullying, or domestic violence.
- **Complex Trauma:** This results from exposure to multiple traumatic events. Examples include being exposed to childhood sexual trauma and then, as an adult, experiencing the loss of a loved one, surviving a natural disaster, combat-related trauma, or duty-related trauma.[9]

It's estimated "that 60–75% of people in North America experience a traumatic event at some point."[10] An article from Medical News Today lists the following as potential causes of trauma, and you may recognize these as the reason for your pit: bullying; harassment; physical, psychological, or sexual abuse; sexual assault; traffic collisions; life-threatening illnesses; sudden loss of a loved one; being attacked; being kidnapped; acts of terrorism; natural disasters; or war.[11]

No matter the *type* of traumatic event you experienced, if you will give the Lord the space in your life, God will use it for good. But it is up to *us,* the ones affected, to choose him over a lifetime of trying to deal with the fallout of trauma in our own power.

The triggers for the pit are different, but God remains the same through it all. And, while you may be still in your own pit of trauma, it is not the end of your story. This is not the final chapter in the book of your life. There is One greater than the pain you feel and the events you experienced, and even though you may not see it now, there is a purpose for your future. Jesus is the key to your healing. He is the source of the power to forgive, the power to love, and the strength to continue fighting.

## Signs You Need to Recognize

We don't list the signs of trauma to wallow in misery or glorify the problems. We do it so we can be aware of what is going on and maybe get a better understanding of why we are feeling certain ways. And, if you are married, it is important for your spouse to know these signs and symptoms so he or she can better support you and validate your feelings as you walk the path of healing. Again, not everyone responds the same way to trauma, but there are some common responses.

I have battled through denial, in the early stages after the blue room, tremendous shame, fear of others, anger, confusion, anxiety, depression, hopelessness, irritability, and difficulty concentrating. These are emotional and psychological responses to trauma you may have felt or may feel in the future. There was a time I had emotional outbursts more frequently than I'd like to admit and wasn't sure how to cope with the feelings I had about my past. I have, at times, isolated myself from others, and certain things trigger flash-backs (nightmares that woke me up) of certain traumas.

Each of these responses can range from mild to severe, and several factors determine how a traumatic event may affect someone, including

- the person's characteristics,
- the presence of other mental health conditions,
- previous exposure to traumatic events,
- the type and characteristics of the event or events, and
- the person's background and approach to handling emotions.[12]

As a law enforcement officer, I was taught to be vigilant, but after some time on the job, I became hypervigilant. This led to various physical symptoms, including migraines, digestive issues (acid reflux), fatigue, racing heartbeats, and sweating. But it also led to hyperarousal and lack of sleep. For a while, I was using alcohol nightly to self-medicate so I could escape the emotions, thoughts, and feelings I had. Substance abuse and other mental health issues are not uncommon outcomes of traumatic events. Knowing the cause of these physical responses to trauma will help you and your support team better address a plan ahead of time and help better understand your behavior.

I personally know men who have experienced different types of trauma from various sources. The men who were involved in combat-related trauma events responded differently than the ones who survived a category five hurricane. The same can go for the men who were abused as children. They respond differently than the men who are involved in other natural disasters, like a major tornado. The key here is that there is no set response, and not everyone will experience post-traumatic stress disorder as a result. It is important for your overall health, spiritual walk, relationships, and career to understand and identify the signs, symptoms, and causes of the emotional responses you are experiencing.

## How to Escape the Pit

*Then they cried to the Lord in their trouble, and he delivered them from their distress. He brought them out of darkness and the shadow of death, and burst their bonds apart. Let them thank the Lord for his steadfast love, for his wondrous works to the children of man! For he shatters the doors of bronze and cuts in two the bars of iron.*

Psalm 107:13–16 esv

Getting out of the pit isn't the most difficult part of the trauma pit. The most difficult part is escaping the pit and not going right into slavery to something else. Joseph was removed from the pit and sold as a slave, and God still used that to his good. The best guarantee for getting out of it for good is to have some strategies in your tool belt.

Take note of the following key points if you are ready to make your pit a place of the past:

1. Win the first battle every day: the alarm clock. Choose whether it will be your first victory or if you will succumb to the allure of comfort and remain in bed.

2. Develop a healthy morning routine. Make your bed, read your Bible, eat a good breakfast. Avoid doomscrolling social media.

3. Talk to someone you trust. It's likely someone who has been healed from what you're battling right now.

4. Manage your time. Time is either a weapon of the enemy or an asset you can use. You don't have

to be in a rush, but you need to begin taking the steps to Jesus.

5. Appreciate the struggle. Your time in the pit can be a curse or a blessing. Decide what you will do with it. Use it for good.

6. Don't fall into the temptation to go from one bad habit to another. Replace bad habits and bad thinking with godly things.

Life has taught me a few things. First, it taught me that self-discipline is one of the most important skills I need to cultivate. Pain has a funny way of teaching that lesson. Let's talk about some practical steps we can use to develop our faith and resilience through self-discipline.

For instance, your alarm clock is not your slave master. Choose to arise with enthusiasm and attack the day by training your body. Keep your body in optimum conditioning, strong, lean, and prepared for anything. Know your limitations and push yourself to give 100 percent in every area of your life. If you want to experience the unconquered life, 100 percent is the minimum! Your mind is a tremendous asset, but your body's conditioning and nutrition feed your brain. You must keep yourself fit to fight for the lives of others and for when you must fight for your life.

Today's challenges will be easier to overcome if you remain disciplined and committed to developing the godly habits needed. The negative influence of others does not have to affect you. Being fit and mentally prepared is your decision, and you can make that decision consistently. If you do, you will be a role model and positive influence on those who have fallen by the wayside with their physical conditioning or in their battles, but you will encourage them and help them get back on track. Your appearance is more than a presence of authority. It is a representation of the amount of respect you have for yourself and your profession. Today, choose to care for your mind, body, and soul.

Second, I learned my healing and escape from the pit didn't *have* to happen overnight and probably wouldn't. It happens in God's perfect timing, and when I learned the necessary lessons in the pit, I would get out. Whether going through pain is a fair method of teaching and learning, I don't know, but we can learn or gripe. I choose to learn. I can't pretend to know what you feel or how to tell you to escape your own pit of trauma, but I can share with you what I have learned through my own experiences. Again, it is critical to note there is no one-size-fits-all solution, with the exception of Jesus. Hope in him, rely on him, and as my friends Evan and Jenny Owens at REBOOT Recovery say, "Depend on your doctors, but abide in Jesus."[13]

It is critical to know what you stand for so that when you are set free from the place of pain and the pit of trauma, you do not bite the bait of something that could enslave you. Remember, your time in pain has taught you something, and you aren't the same person you were before. You are stronger, wiser, and more powerful. To this day, these are some things that have helped me get out of the trauma pit and navigate the other challenges of trauma that have come my way over the years.

1. Know what you believe and stand for and stick to it.

2. Be content with the things you have and grateful for the people in your life.

3. Journal about people, situations, and things you have to be grateful for, including certain challenges during the day. Take notes on what you could have done better in any conflict you faced and plan how you will approach the next day.

4.  Find a mentor. Godly mentors are a gift. We do
    not need people who will agree with everything
    we say but who will challenge us, hold our feet to
    the fire, and guide us through struggles. I have a
    select few godly men in my life I can count on at
    any hour of the day or night.

5.  Develop the right mindset. If your mindset isn't
    in the right frame, you will be fighting an uphill
    battle. Our beliefs determine the trajectory of our
    thoughts. Our thoughts feed the words we speak.
    Our words dictate our actions, and our consistent
    actions develop the outcomes we experience in
    our life. Mindset matters! We are not victims. We
    are victors!

6.  Breathe! While it sounds like a no-brainer, cer-
    tain breathing techniques we will cover later in
    the book can help you calm your heart rate and
    get your body back into a balanced state.

Now, you need to find what works for you. If you are
still fighting a battle alone, the first key is to find someone
who is qualified to walk you through that battle to victory.
And while God does work miracles in our lives, he often
uses other people to facilitate those things. Seek someone
who is qualified to help you. Well-meaning people, including friends, family, and other Christians in your life, will say
things like, "Just trust God for your healing." Or, with the
best intentions, they may say, "Just give it to God!" These
statements have deeper, more significant meanings, but the
statements themselves are cliché and seldom beneficial to
individuals in a place of pain.

Daily journaling, time spent studying God's Word,
prayer, and godly mentors will be the core of your toolkit for
escaping the pit of trauma. It's not always going to be easy,
smooth, or even pretty. You're going to have rough days, and

some days you will feel like you are regressing and falling back. When you are fighting your way out of the pit, community is a key element. They will be with you as you take this journey to heal. They will walk with you through the good times, and their value will be proven immeasurable in the hard times. Find people in your community who have experienced pain and healing and spend time with them. There are a number of resources at your disposal. Consider these organizations as tools in your battle:

- Mighty Oaks Programs (www.MightyOaksPrograms.com)
- Celebrate Recovery (www.CelebrateRecovery.com)
- REBOOT Recovery (www.RebootRecovery.org)

## Unconquered Code #2

Recognize you are in control of yourself and that you are in control of no one else.

## Battle Action Step

Seek a godly mentor who can walk with you on your journey to live unconquered.

## Discussion

1. How can you start your day off victoriously?
2. What are five things you can do to no longer have negative emotional ties to past pain?
3. In what ways can you better manage your time?

## Prayer

*Heavenly Father, you know where I am in my life right now, and you know better than I do how I have been affected by the events in my life. But this battle is yours, and I cannot do it alone. Give me the strength to fight and deliver me from the distress I am facing. I praise you for your love, for your works, and for delivering me from the pit of trauma. Amen.*

*I don't regret the difficulties I experienced;*
*I think they helped me to become the person*
*I am today. I feel the way a warrior must feel*
*after years of training: he doesn't remember the*
*details of everything he learned, but he knows*
*how to strike when the time is right.*

PAULO COELHO[14]

# NOW IS THE TIME

*"Understand your past,
live this moment,
dream your future."*

MAXIME LAGACÉ[15]

I sat across from the pastor of our church and one of the board members. "What do you want to be, Adam?" the board member asked me. This was during a time when I was unemployed, working odd jobs to make ends meet. Amber was unable to work due to pregnancy complications with our third child.

"I want to be a youth pastor," I replied reluctantly. I was not sure if that was what I really wanted, but it sounded good. After all, that's what "ministry" is, right? No. It's not. It's one aspect of ministry. But as I sat there talking to these men, I realized how lost I really was.

"Here's the deal, Adam, and I'm not sure you've ever had someone tell you this. But you need to man up. That's what you need to do. Your wife is home without any income right now, and you're wanting to be a youth pastor. Is that really what you want?"

The next thing out of my mouth revealed what the issue was in my heart: "Nothing ever works out for me. I get what you're trying to say. But you don't understand what I've had to try to overcome."

"So you think you're a victim then, is that it? Do you think all the stuff that you've experienced in life happened to just you? Nobody else?" My pastor sat quietly, knowing good and well what I needed to hear was coming right down the pipe.

"You know what, I don't want to do this. I appreciate you taking the time to talk with me, but this really isn't helpful. I get what you're saying, and it worked. Thank you for your time."

I got up from the table and walked away. I was angry, beyond angry. Who did he think he was to talk to me like that? Nobody talks to me like that.

After a few days, I settled down and realized he was right, which was hard to admit even to myself. I decided to call him because, deep down, I knew I had a lot of stuff to work on.

This wasn't easy for me to apologize. "You don't know everything about me, but you were right. I mean, you are right. You called me out. I've been going about this all wrong, and I am not sure what to do next. But I do know I want to be a cop. That's my next step. Thank you for challenging me."

A few months later, I swore in as a law enforcement officer and never looked back. The person who I was at that meeting with the board member, the person who lacked confidence, who lived to sabotage his own life, had died.

I finally understand why it took me so long to become a man. It was because for most of my life, I was trying to live while dragging the past with me through it all. It's just not going to work, no matter how bad you want it to. It never does. Living in the past weakens you and keeps you from growing, but the point is to learn from it all. Take something away from every experience and learn from it. But trying to live with the baggage of yesterday only creates a toxic cycle of self-sabotage behavior. It's in our minds first, and what we think is all rooted in what we believe. No thought remains except those we believe and entertain.

My issue was my victim mentality. I saw everything that ever happened in my life as something out to get me instead of having the right perspective of life. I think it is normal for us to want to feel good, and if we're not made whole from past experiences, especially those that were trauma related, we can begin a negative cycle of thinking and behaviors that lead to constant self-sabotage. That's the only "fruit" that comes from living in the past. It's toxic, deadly, and a dream destroyer.

So many people had tried to help me, but I was too blind to see it. I was too hurt to see it. It had been seven years since I began working on forgiving the man who hurt me as a five-year-old boy and everyone who condoned, dismissed, and played a part in the church lady debacle as a teenager. So much hate, so much bitterness, so much resentment weighed me down. I wasn't trying to relive my past, but I was trying to heal myself by finding different ways to feel good instead of dealing with the root of the pain in my life.

Living unconquered isn't determined by the number of wins or losses in life. It's determined by your resolve to keep fighting even when you're outnumbered, out of ammo, out of breath, out of energy, and out of resources. No matter what, you keep taking the fight to life. Trying to live in the past isn't always about holding on to the painful experiences you've endured or the failed relationships, businesses, or dead dreams. Sometimes it means taking your response to those points of pain and attempting to self-medicate in the present moments when your pain resurfaces due to other external conflicts. Are you living for eternity right now, or are you still holding on to whatever God has promised to set you free from if you will only surrender it to him?

## Created for More

If you're carrying burdens in your life right now, this is a great place to stop and take a breather. Rest a bit. Before destroying my knees, I loved running nearby trails. On every trail I've run, there are benches and places to get water. This is a bench spot for you and me to take a second to rest. Your life is not defined by the burdens you've carried, but it will be remembered by the ones you never released.

I'm not sure why I tried to self-medicate instead of seeking help sooner. Still, I know I learned a lot from my battles, and I am grateful for every lesson I've learned along the way. I am reminded that God can use our mess to create a place for us, propel us into our destiny, and help us discover our purpose here in this life.

During various phases of training in law enforcement, we would have to drag a dummy that weighs the equivalent of a human being. Dragging those dummies is easy for a short distance, but then it becomes more difficult. Think about carrying two hundred extra pounds on your back for ten feet, then twenty, then the length of a football field. Now you have to carry it across town, up and down flights of stairs, take it to bed, to the shower; it's part of your everyday life. At some point, you will break down. That's the breaking point. That's why Jesus said, "Come to me, all who labor and are heavy laden, and I will give you rest" (Matthew 11:28 ESV). He's already paid the price for everything we carry today, so I suppose that makes us thieves if we take possession of something he paid for.

It took getting to my breaking point to realize there was a better way to live. During my time in law enforcement, I would often have vivid dreams of work-related situations. One recurring dream would be a gunfight, and when I pulled the trigger on my firearm, it either did nothing or the bullet drooped like syrup. In some instances, the bullets did nothing to the person trying to kill me. I knew these dreams meant I needed to go to the gun range and train. The instructors agreed, saying these dreams were normal.

But during my last year in law enforcement, I remember two particularly vivid dreams. In the first dream, I was lying in a coffin inside a funeral home chapel. To this day, when I talk about it or write about it, I begin to smell the same fragrances from that dream. It was very real to me. I heard the murmurs of a group of people talking nearby but couldn't make out what they were saying. All I remember is hearing them talk, the smells, and then a thunderous sound, like the *snap* of two fingers, followed by a voice saying, "Did you do what I created you to do?" I awakened, startled by the dream, but carried on with my life.

The second dream came a few months later. It was similar, but this time, the top of the coffin was closed. I was being lowered into the ground, and I could hear dirt being thrown onto the coffin. Again, that thunderous *snap* followed by the same voice asking, "Did you do what I created you to do?"

I am no dream interpreter, and maybe it was just a fluke caused by something I experienced or ate beforehand. But what if it was God? What if he was trying to get my attention through those dreams, when I was not distracted or in my own way?

Allow me to pose a question to you: Are you doing what God created you to do? If you're living in the past and carrying the burdens you've been commanded to give to him, chances are, no, you're not. Jesus came to give us life and life to the fullest (see John 10:10), and living with unaddressed wounds isn't living to the fullest. Self-sabotage isn't living to the fullest. Living life to the fullest is entirely possible when we place our faith in the right source and when we acknowledge the presence of pain and have the courage to begin healing.

When you get to the point where you are ready to begin living the life he created you to live, it means dying to who you used to be. No longer burdened by the past, no longer shamed by sin, no longer a prisoner of a victim mentality. No, you are now more than a conqueror and his child. It's time to learn how to live victoriously.

## Primary Growth Inhibitors

A lot of things in the kingdom of God are the opposite of the things in his world. Jesus said if you want to be first, you must be last, and if you want to lead, you must serve, to name two. You would think that carrying the weight of our past would mean we get stronger. It is exhausting and one of the biggest blocks to your personal growth I know of.

I grew up working alongside my dad, repairing vehicles that had been involved in automobile collisions and towing vehicles from crash scenes or after a driver had been arrested. Once, after midnight, I remember Dad coming to wake me up. I knew what that meant. For me, it was game time. I was too young to drive just yet, but time with Dad, especially running the wreckers, was so much fun. Plus, I knew I would likely get to talk to our local law enforcement. They called Dad to tow this particular vehicle because a man had been arrested for driving under the influence.

To this day, I don't know the man's name, but I can see his face in my mind. He was arrested wearing a military dress blue uniform. I was just a kid, and while he was arrested in uniform, he left his uniform cover in the vehicle. I put it on and looked in the mirror and further resolved that my path would be in the military. I knew this driver's behavior didn't represent military values, but his behavior didn't deter me from my dream to serve in the military. Deep down in my heart, my future plans all involved a dream to serve a career in the United States Armed Forces. Seeing this man's uniform was the closest I'd been. I wanted to serve my country as a United States Marine.

I ran into the shop one day where my dad was working, and I told him, "I'm going to be a Marine, Dad. That's what I want to do." He wasn't critical of my decision, and I am grateful to him for his approach. He has guided me, or at least tried to, even when I was too stubborn to listen.

"Son, that's good, but how's that going to help you when you get out? What will you do?"

He posed a good question. So I went on to tell him, "I am going to become a lawyer in the Marines and retire. That's my plan." I went all in. As a teenager who had, for most of my life, lacked any type of real direction, I finally knew where I was heading. So, I began talking to recruiters, reading everything I could on what to expect, learning what it meant to be a Marine, and training every day. This was my path, and I was excited. For once, something was working out, and I had my eyes on a dream. I had it all figured out.

But things changed when, sometime shortly after my sixteenth birthday, I noticed severe pain in my left ear and went to a local specialist. The doctor said there was a cyst on my left eardrum and that I would require surgery to remove it. The doctors had to cut my scalp behind my left ear, from the top of my ear toward the bottom of my ear. While they did remove the cyst, it left a small hole in my left eardrum, which proved to be the demise of my dream to become a United States Marine about five years later. After several attempts to obtain a waiver for my ear issues so I could enlist, I was required to take a hearing test at the Military Entrance Processing Station in Montgomery, Alabama, which I failed. My left ear sustained significant damage, and hearing loss was apparent from the cyst removal and numerous ear infections.

"Davis, I'm sorry, but as much as you want the Marines, the Marines don't want you," the recruiter said. "You've been PDQ'd."

"What's that mean, sir?" I asked him.

"It means you will never be in the United States Armed Forces. You've been permanently disqualified."

I didn't take no for an answer. I began writing letters to politicians and the highest-ranking Marines at the time but to no avail. Five years passed, and I finally accepted my fate. As much as I had wanted to serve my country, it was a dream I had to bury. It was time to dream a new dream.

Trying to live in the past is like watering a dead plant. You know it's dead. It's obvious. All you're doing is wasting energy and resources you could better use in the present and in preparing for your future. Continuing to nurture dead plants, or living in the past, creates frustration, and I was frustrated. So one dream didn't work out for me, but I learned a lot about myself, lessons I wouldn't realize until years later.

I've come to believe there is no such thing as coincidence, but there are patterns on the timeline of our lives to pay attention to. How was I supposed to plan if all I knew was pain and dreams destroyed? It's disheartening to try to plan for the future when all you can see at every mile marker in your life is a place of defeat. It's hard to have enthusiasm when another dream comes up in your heart, and it's hard to have the faith to keep on living. I learned that sometimes, our dreams don't die, and our failure isn't always the end because it is all a divine redirection to align us with our God-given destiny.

We all have different dreams, some we are more vested in than others. But I know if I had continued living with the past as the standard for my life, I would have lived in the past until I died there. It's a fact. If you are moving backward, you're not growing, and if you aren't growing, you're dying at a faster rate than you are living. In high school and college, we are taught history lessons so we can understand more about who we are as a nation, as human beings, and about the events of the world. History is supposed to be a lesson, not a modern-day, breaking-news headline. Everything you've experienced, everything that has occurred in your life has prepared you for the present. It's time to discover hope again but this time with no reluctance for the possibility of what God has in store for you.

I never had the privilege of serving in our nation's military. Nevertheless, I have learned that God still uses the desires of our hearts when we let him take our burdens away. I coauthored two books with Lt. Col. Dave Grossman (US Army, Retired): *Bulletproof Marriage: A 90-Day Devotional* and *On Spiritual Combat: 30 Missions for Victorious Warfare.* Because of Lt. Col. Grossman's military and law enforcement connections, those two books have touched tens of thousands of lives, including men and women in the United States Armed Forces. And in 2021, I coauthored a book, *Behind the Lines: 365 Daily Challenges for Military Personnel,* with former Force Recon Marine and MMA Champion Chad Robichaux. Chad is the founder of Mighty Oaks Foundation, which focuses on helping military veterans and first responders overcome trauma through a faith-based program. Because of Chad and his service in the Marines, this book has touched numerous lives of servicemen and women, including men and women from the United States Marines, United States Army, United States Navy, United States Air Force, and United States Coast Guard. The Lord truly uses all things for his good! I couldn't serve with them, but through God's divine direction and providence, he has used my gifts and relationships to touch the men and women who *do* serve.

## Faith-Fueled Strategic Action

I am a slow learner, and I don't say that remotely jokingly. Thinking about it makes me cringe because I created so much pain for myself and others before I learned this reality. When I began the application process to become a law enforcement officer in the state of Alabama, I weighed nearly three hundred pounds. At a height of six feet tall, I was morbidly obese and in terrible health. It had been a long time since I had done any type of workout or even had any concern with the type of food I ate. I was fat, out of shape, and lazy.

I applied to the police department in September 2008, and the entire hiring process took almost one year to the day I was sworn in as an officer. During the first few weeks of being hired as a police officer, I was introduced to two men, both veterans of the United States Armed Forces, one from the Army, the other from the Navy. These men were the best of the best, and our department was privileged to have them in the training division. They motivated me to take actions that led to positive changes and challenged me at every turn. They not only helped me change my body to meet the demands of the law enforcement profession, but they also trained me to stay alive and survive on patrol and through any potential effects of the job. I lost around sixty pounds from the day I began at the police department and graduated from the police academy. My nutrition was still not the best, but my calorie intake had been drastically reduced.

From barely running one and a half miles a day, I was running around ten miles a day, but I did not stretch properly. One day after a run during pre-academy training, I felt a sharp pain in my right hip. I tried to walk it off, but it only worsened. After seeing a few doctors, it was determined that I had torn my iliotibial (IT) band on the right side of my body.

My memory of the medical treatment is not that clear, but I remember it involved crutches, stretching, and shots in my hip that hurt like the dickens. At the time I was hired, as

I am sure is still the case today, each candidate had to attend the academy within so many days of being hired. Toward the end of my recovery period, I began to run more than I should have in hopes that I would get into the next academy class on time. My instructors told me, "When you show up for the day one PT test, don't go all out like you usually do. Just do enough to pass." They knew I had been pushing it, trying to make it. But my pride got the better of me, and I pushed myself too hard and reinjured the IT band on my right side. I tried to play it off so the instructors didn't see, but getting up several flights of stairs to my room, running, and completing all the other physical activities required during the academy became nearly impossible.

One of the first mornings during our PT session, one of the instructors noticed my limp and that I was slower than everyone else. "You can't run, Davis? What's your deal!"

I knew if I lied to him, it would not end well for me. So I told him. "I hurt my right hip, sir."

"Fine!" he said with a growl. "We have another work-out you can do while everyone else runs since you can't run."

Something in my mind said, *This isn't going to be an easy out from running*, and I was correct. "Davis, get on the ground in a push-up position. When I blow this whistle, you start doing push-ups, and when I blow it again, you begin doing sit-ups, and we will rotate those two until your class finishes running."

Now, I know when you are reading this, those words probably come through your mind like an elementary school teacher reading stories to a young class. But that was not the case. This particular instructor wanted to be dang sure I was truly injured and not just lazy. He spoke at high volumes with a lot of energy. Those who have attended basic training or police academy are probably giggling right now because you know exactly what said he was saying.

On day three of my academy training in Selma, Alabama, the instructors called me out of class and told me to head to the colonel's office. I limped in, and after he gave me permission, I sat down. I don't remember this man's name, but I will never forget what he told me.

"Davis, I see you are here from the Dothan Police Department. Since you came here with an old injury and this injury did not originate from training while present at this academy, we have to send you home." He couldn't be serious. "But I want you to take this as a learning opportunity. You came in here, and you knew your limits. If you are going to make it in law enforcement, it's going to require you to know your limits and work within those limits. You get hurt, or worse, when you try to operate outside your limits."

It was another lesson I had to learn the hard way. We cannot change yesterday, but we can improve today and again tomorrow. We can't undo our sins, mistakes, or bad decisions. Instead of continuing to dwell on what I had done, I made a decision to improve every day. I was determined to make this work.

The following day after arriving back at the department, I was sitting in the training room when the chief of police walked up to me. He told me the city had to send me home and that I would be terminated until I could get in the academy. After being at home for a few days, the chief's secretary called me and told me I needed to come in. They said I would be put on light duty until I could fully heal and then attend an academy in southwest Alabama. Being sent home from the academy was terrible, but it proved to be a great lesson. I needed to learn to operate within my limitations. Know them, push them, but live within them.

Sitting in the training room with crutches and unable to train with the rest of the class felt a lot like the punch in the gut I felt when they told me I could never be in the military. I began thinking about why I applied to be a law enforcement officer in the first place. I had to do some deep soul-searching because this wasn't about me anymore. This was about my family, and I had no choice but to overcome the obstacle. Being permanently disqualified from serving in the military prepared me to respond in the right way to this challenge to fight for my law enforcement career. It was a survive-or-die moment.

## An Einstein Moment

I recently saw a meme on social media that said, "Live. Learn. Hope." It was so simple, yet deeply profound, and it made me want to read more about it. When I did some research, I discovered Albert Einstein is actually credited with saying, "Learn from yesterday, live for today, hope for tomorrow. The important thing is not to stop questioning."

You have a choice. We all have the gift of choice. We can choose to be grateful, or we can choose to be miserable. Gratitude has a powerful way of changing our emotions and thoughts for the better. It requires that we begin to shift our focus from all the events of our past and stop and say, "I am grateful for each experience. I learned something from everything I've been through in life, and I am going to be better and stronger." Put the past in a box right now and write on the shipping label, "To God. Nonreturnable." It's not yours anymore. You got what you needed from it. Now it's time to grow! I know there's a lot of pain there, but stuff it into that box too. Keep the good memories, and let those be lessons too.

What good is tomorrow without hope? That's a familiar feeling and used to be a recurring thought for me. We can put our hope for tomorrow in opportunities and dreams, or we can think eternally. How is what we are doing right now going to impact eternity for others or ourselves? Recently a friend of mine sent me a video of John Bevere speaking on the topic of multiplication. In the sermon, Mr. Bevere states that our stewardship isn't about maintaining; it's about multiplying.[16] We can't be labeled good stewards if we only maintain what we've been given, so we must use it to grow it. This is a moment for you to begin doing that, right now. Think about what opportunities and relationships you have in your life.

Dr. Annie Tanasugarn published an article for PsychCentral.com on the topic of living in the past and present. One of the best ways to live in the present, according to Tanasugarn, is to accept the past. It's done. The other is to establish boundaries and be more selective about whom we allow into our lives. My favorite is mindfulness. Learning how to calm our minds and thoughts when we are emotionally triggered is a skill we must learn and develop.[17] To help with this, I use something called "box breathing."[18] Now, box breathing is not new, and in fact, it is used by many first responders and military, including US Navy SEALS. I remember, during officer survival training in law enforcement, being taught a variation of this method of calming our bodies and minds. It looks like this:

1. Sit up straight with your feet flat on the floor.

2. Close your eyes and inhale for four counts.

3. Hold your breath for four counts.

4. Exhale for four counts.

5. Repeat.

When I talk about mindfulness, it means being present. We can't be present if we're always in a panic. If I find myself experiencing some negative emotion because of a series of thoughts or if I feel a panic attack ensuing, calm breathing is the first thing I go to. During my breathing exercise, I focus on a particular Bible verse, maybe something I read that morning. And if you really want the most benefits from this tool, begin your day with this breathing exercise. It also has helped me tremendously to prepare for sleep.

I want to provide you with the most resources and tools possible to help you live the unconquered life. It is possible. It is a reality, and it should become the declaration of every person. During a discussion with my children a few years ago, we were talking about how certain social situations cause feelings of anxiety or nervousness. It was a late-night conversation and one that I particularly enjoyed. One of my kids looked at me and said, "What do I do when I feel this way?"

"Just give it to God."

That's it. That was my response. While it was well-meaning, it was terrible advice. My kid knew it, too, responding, "But how, Daddy?"

Well, this is how. That's what I am sharing with you, the ways I've helped my own family and many first responders, including myself. When you are feeling overwhelmed or if you find yourself beginning to drift back into an old, past mentality or if you are becoming anxious about the future, arrest your thoughts. Calm your mind. De-escalate your body by meditating on a Scripture verse, box breathing, and fixing your focus back on the present moment.

Christian clichés aren't effective in dealing with deep pain. We need to be shown how to do this, not told to do it. I get that. It means we recognize that Jesus is the way, the truth, and the life, but he will not force us to give up our burdens. It's up to us. This requires us to learn some effective ways to manage negative emotions and learn from the past. The gospel is practical if we will apply it in our lives. The time to start learning from your past is now.

## Unconquered Code #3

Live in the present, hope for the future, and learn from the past.

## Battle Action Step

Practice the box-breathing technique for five minutes a day every day over the next week. Document how it positively affects you.

## Discussion

1. What are some lessons you can learn from your past experiences?

2. How can you better live in the present moment?

3. What are some strategic faith-fueled action steps you can take to discover hope for the future?

## Prayer

*Heavenly Father, thank you for every moment in my life. I am learning to rejoice in everything, even the pain! You take all things and work them for good, and today, I choose to give you every moment of my life and ask you to redeem those painful places. I place my hope in you for the future and give you today in gratitude. Amen.*

*Forgiveness does not mean ignoring what has been done or putting a false label on an evil act. It means, rather, that the evil act no longer remains as a barrier to the relationship. Forgiveness is a catalyst creating the atmosphere necessary for a fresh start and a new beginning.*

MARTIN LUTHER KING JR.[19]

## PRINCIPLE #4

# FAITH TO FORGIVE

*"If you forgive other people when they sin against you,*
*your heavenly Father will also forgive you.*
*But if you do not forgive others their sins,*
*your Father will not forgive your sins."*

<small>Matthew 6:14–15 niv</small>

Forgiveness is a choice, and it is seldom a one-time event. It doesn't mean you forget the pain someone else caused you, and it doesn't mean you become a doormat for the offender to hurt you again. You can choose to forgive or refuse forgiveness. Now, you can also choose to eat fast food every meal every single day for the rest of your life, but chances are, you will have a lot of health issues.

I've been on both sides of this issue of forgiveness. For more than two decades, I carried hate and resentment in my heart. And if I am going to be honest about everything, I may as well tell you I've dealt with them since then too. But now, instead of it taking me twenty years to forgive, I am quicker to forgive. What I've discovered is that the closer I am to the person who hurt me, the harder it is to forgive—not because

I don't love them but because I would never hurt them the way they hurt me.

If you're not careful, allowing resentment to grow in your life will lead to selfish behavior. Unaddressed pain begets more pain. I want to help you see the benefits of forgiveness, how it is really something that benefits you, and how to forgive. As I worked with my team on preparing this book, I learned that a lot of it really is about forgiveness. That's quite possibly the biggest and most important step in walking this life unconquered.

Shortly after the release of my first book, *Behind the Badge: 365 Daily Devotions for Law Enforcement*, I went to a major book retailer to find my book on the shelf. Having my book in a brick-and-mortar bookstore was a big deal to me, and I wanted to see my book and pray over it. But I didn't want to appear odd by standing and gawking at my book, so I walked up and down the aisle, pretending to look for the next life-changing book to read. What no one knew was that, internally, my heart was in the midst of a fiery prayer for the next person who would see it and for God to use it to have an impact on their life for eternity. Of course, God doesn't answer all prayers as quickly as he answered that prayer, but sometimes, God surprises us.

As I made my way down the Christian living section in the store, a young man was standing near my book. So, I struck up a conversation with him.

"There sure is a lot to choose from."

"Yeah, there is," the gentleman replied. "Not sure what to get though. I am looking for a good devo." He seemed like a nice guy who genuinely wanted to find this book for which he was searching.

"Hey, you may enjoy this one."

As a new author, I shamelessly handed him a copy of my book. As soon as his hand took possession of the book, his entire demeanor changed. He went from being open to our conversation to looking like he was ready to fight.

He looked me straight in my eyes and said with a stern yet quiet tone, "You have no idea how much I hate cops. I hate them. They have ruined my life. My girl left me for a cop, not to mention the number of times they have mistreated me so much. I hate them."

Rage had overtaken this man completely. His eyes changed from a relaxed and friendly look to stern, pointed eyebrows and an angry, intimidating countenance. I noticed his hands as he clenched his fists, and sweat was beading on his forehead. Initially, as I observed all his signs of anger, I thought, *There's no way I am about to have to fight this guy in the Christian living section of a bookstore*. Now, I am not afraid of a fight, but there's a time to fight and time to de-escalate. I used some verbal judo skills I learned as a negotiator to help calm the man and de-escalate a situation I could never have predicted.

Before I responded, I whispered a quick prayer for direction and wisdom. It's what I call 911 prayers. Think about it like this: when you call 911, you aren't calling to get acquainted. You need help, and you needed it thirty minutes ago. God will answer your 911 prayers. What followed my prayer and the entire encounter after his animated and brash expression of hatred for law enforcement is something I will never forget.

"Listen, man, I get it, okay. I've been mistreated and, yes, by some fellow law enforcement officers, fellow brothers and sisters in Christ, and family. But hate will kill you. So I want to challenge you, right here, right now, in love, as a brother in Christ. Is that okay with you?"

Tears began to well up in his eyes.

"Yeah, hate is ripping me apart inside. I can't believe I am sharing this with you; I don't even know you."

"Whether you read this book or not, we both read the Bible. But I want you to take this book, and every time you look at it or see it, let it be a reminder for you to pray for cops. Not because you support all of them or even like them but because we both choose to love them and everyone else. Love is not an option, but hate is. Hate is the bait of hell and a gateway for the enemy's authority to control your life. So take this book, and when you read it, let it be a reminder to pray for them. Wouldn't that spark more change than hate?"

Tears began running down both cheeks as he began to weep. It became apparent through his behavior and tone of voice that he had been wrestling with this for some time.

"I've never had anyone challenge my hate that way. I promise to pray for them daily. How do I pray for these cops? Can you help me?"

Meeting this man was a pivotal moment for me that changed my perspective on how I could best serve my brothers and sisters in law enforcement. It was here I learned I could stand in the gap between the world that hated them and those who continue to serve. I could do this by helping others learn how to pray for law enforcement and love them well through a relationship with Jesus. This was not only a mission for me but for every man and woman who follows Jesus. They just needed to know *how* to pray for law enforcement officers.

I pointed out a few strategies to the man in the bookstore, some methods I used myself and some I previously shared with others who asked me the same question.

"First, recognize God as your Father. His love is perfect love, and if we hate anyone, his love is not in us. Second, recognize law enforcement officers as his children; though not all have the same faith or beliefs, we are all made in God's image. They are his as we are his. Third, recognize we are all human beings, imperfect and incredibly wretched. We need the blood of Jesus to cleanse us, and without him, we are nothing. Fourth, I have a list of practical things you can cover in your prayer time as you intercede for law enforcement throughout the coming days. Things like their mental well-being, physical well-being, spiritual well-being, the families they have, their relationships, finances, and some internal issues among agencies, sort of like the business side of policing. But I have also used a method of praying you may find helpful, and it will help you in growing in your relationship with Jesus."

I handed him some notes I scribbled on a partially used napkin and gave him some parting encouragement. He expressed deep remorse for his heart toward law enforcement. He even said he would be working on forgiving those who had mistreated him. We prayed together, and I purchased the book and gifted it to him before we went our separate ways, and we even stayed in touch for a while afterward.

Now, I do not believe in coincidences, only God moments. And this God moment began a mission for me to encourage not only law enforcement but also those whom they serve. It helped me realize how powerful forgiveness can be and that even Christians deal with this issue. I don't make a habit of striking up conversations with strangers in bookstores, believe it or not, but this is one I will always be grateful happened.

## What Is Forgiveness?

The man I met in the bookstore was telling me how much he hated law enforcement, but he was also telling me there was a pain in his life that he associated with this group of men and women. In that aisle, right when he was confronted with love, he had a decision to make. Would he choose to continue resenting those who caused him pain, or would he let go of resentment? He chose to accept peace, move on with his life, and grow in his relationship with God. It was obvious by his initial response that he had allowed feelings of anger, hostility, and rage to overtake his life by holding on to grudges and refusing to forgive.

Forgiveness isn't letting the offender off the hook or condoning what they did to you. It also doesn't mean you have to reenter a relationship with the person who hurt you, as in the case of domestic or sexual abuse. However, it does mean you release the resentment and desire for revenge and no longer allow that offense to control your life.

Think about it like this: if you are armed with a firearm and your job is to patrol a city as a police officer, refusing to forgive someone is like carrying a firearm with an empty magazine. There's no firepower. You can't use it except as a paperweight. That's all it's good for, and it only causes you pain if you are in a gunfight. But we are born into a nature of sin, and therefore, it is not always easy to forgive. Sometimes holding a grudge is much easier for us than letting go of those negative feelings. It's easier to hate than to love and easier to resent than to forgive.

Forgiveness requires faith, and if we profess to be followers of Jesus, it is not an option or suggestion. Holding on to grudges and being resentful only further deepens the roots of hostility and hatred in our hearts, further dividing us from the presence of God. Notice I didn't say it separates us from his love because his love is available freely whenever we are ready. But we cannot walk in the fullness of life without knowing the power of forgiveness.

## You Can Forgive Even When You Don't Feel Like It

When I think about the topic of forgiveness, I go back to what Jesus said to Peter. In Matthew 18:21 it reads, "Peter came up and said to him, 'Lord, how often will my brother sin against me, and I forgive him? As many as seven times?'" (ESV). In rabbinic discussions, it was the general consensus that a person could be forgiven three times, but after the fourth offense, forgiveness was not an option. Peter assumed a suggested seven times would be a bighearted approach to this issue, but in verse 22, "Jesus said to him, 'I do not say to you seven times, but seventy-seven times.'" If I think about it in terms of whether someone is deserving of forgiveness, it makes it all the more difficult to process. Jesus wasn't suggesting that seventy-seven times was the maximum amount of forgiveness allowed. Rather, he was saying that we have been forgiven more than we will ever be required to forgive. Forgiveness is freely given to us, and therefore, we must forgive.

Faith is more than a topic to discuss in church or small groups. It's an action, something we must put to work, and there's no better place to practice it than by forgiving others. Sometimes, it means forgiving yourself. In Matthew 6:14–15, Jesus said, "For if you forgive others their trespasses, your heavenly Father will also forgive you, but if you do not forgive others their trespasses, neither will your Father forgive your trespasses" (ESV). This means we must forgive to be forgiven, and that's tough. It certainly does require faith to do something like forgiving someone who hurt us deeply.

During a particularly difficult time in my life, I was unfaithful to my wife. Still, she stayed with me. I recall one discussion with my wife about my actions and I asked her why she forgave me, why she loved me, and why she remained by my side. "Because Jesus has forgiven me of so much, how can I not forgive you?" Her response was so incredibly profound, it stunned me. I didn't know how to respond. It didn't mean everything was swept under the rug, but it did make room for reconciliation and healing in our marriage.

You see, when we choose to forgive the most painful offenses, we not only demonstrate what Jesus commanded us to do, but we also exemplify the love of God to others. It's easy to forgive someone for cutting you off in traffic, but it's much more challenging to forgive a spouse who hurt you deeply.

My relationship with Amber has taught me so much over our two-plus decades together. Her love for me has been a constant reminder of how God loves us: perfectly and unconditionally. That's not to say she hasn't been frustrated or angry with me at times. I know she has, but she chose love and forgiveness. She has demonstrated Ephesians 4:32, "Be kind to one another, tenderhearted, forgiving one another, even as God in Christ forgave you" (NKJV).

We have the option to choose, even taking into account what Jesus said in the book of Matthew. We can choose to reject God's grace, forgiveness, and love. It's a painful place to live, and it's a hard way to live, but it is our choice. However, if you want to live unconquered and to the fullest, if you want to experience forgiveness for yourself, it means taking the first step: not forgiving because someone is deserving but, rather, doing so out of obedience to God and doing so in faith. You don't have to understand it or agree with it, but you must take the first step and let God do what only he can do with the rest.

When I began the journey of healing from trauma, it began with forgiveness. I didn't feel any different the first time I whispered, "I forgive them," than I did the moments prior when I hated them. But every day, I chose forgiveness. I still choose forgiveness, and I am not sure how long it took me to get to the point where I no longer had hate in my heart toward the offenders in my life, but I know, eventually, faith took over, and healing became reality.

You may experience something totally different. In fact, you may feel totally free after the first time you pray for those who hurt you and forgive them. That's the beauty of God's grace. It meets us all in our walk of life in different ways, but the result is the same: redemption. We cannot judge the offenders and forgive them at the same time. We must choose whether we will be the judge or submit those tasks to God, and we do what he commanded us to do by forgiving and loving them.

## Benefits of Forgiveness

In my twenties, I was diagnosed with high blood pressure and put on medication to help regulate it back into a healthy range. It never occurred to me that withholding forgiveness for so long could be the root cause. I later discovered there are a number of health issues that can surface as a result of negative emotions, including resentment and hate. Things like worry, anxiety, resentment, and bitterness can literally make you physically sick,[20] and I had no idea. As I searched for scientific evidence to support my belief that forgiveness improves physical health, I discovered the Mayo Clinic released a study on the benefits of forgiveness. Here are a few of the benefits mentioned in their article:

- Healthier relationships
- Improved mental health
- Less anxiety, stress, and hostility
- Lower blood pressure
- Fewer symptoms of depression
- A stronger immune system
- Improved heart health
- Improved self-esteem[21]

There it was in black and white. My grudges were literally destroying my body. It's not something I can easily comprehend, but I have experienced it. When someone says to me, "You have to forgive them, Adam," my initial reaction is, "No, I don't! I don't have to do anything." That's just a self-defense mechanism. By hardening my heart and shutting down, it makes me feel like refusing to forgive others somehow helps me, but it doesn't. In fact, it's the opposite.

I want to walk through this together. Think about any issue in your life for which you have not forgiven the offender, even if the offender is you. Now, I want you to consider, right now, how it is beneficial to you to continue harboring that resentment and holding on to those grudges. Close your eyes and take a moment to think through this with me. Once you are there, open your eyes, and we will proceed together.

As you visualize the face of the person who harmed you, think about how Jesus would respond to their offense. Has he forgiven them, and has he forgiven you? In this position, although it is a personal choice and decision, if you refuse to forgive, you are forfeiting the benefits you could experience over time as a result of letting go. Letting go doesn't mean you're accepting the pain as a permanent part of your life. Rather, you are choosing to forgive and live a healthier life mentally, physically, and spiritually. When I did this initially, I began to grow spiritually by leaps and bounds because forgiveness was the key to opening my personal prison. I was set free and no longer bound by those things. All the anger, all the rage, all those heavy negative emotions no longer weighed me down.

I can hear some folks asking, "What about (insert offense and offender)?" I was that person, so I can empathize with you on this issue. And I suppose, if you can't take one step to forgive, you can at least empathize or put yourself in their shoes. You don't do this to become like them or try to embrace their behavior. You do it so you can draw closer to a place of forgiveness.

## Practical Steps for Practicing Forgiveness

When Jesus taught us how to pray in the book of Matthew and Luke, it was evident that forgiveness was a two-way street and something we are to practice daily. He said it like this: "Forgive us our debts, as we also have forgiven our debtors" (Matthew 6:12 NIV). How can we possibly be forgiven if we choose each day to live with resentment and hate? We cannot! To be forgiven we must choose to forgive in faith, as an act of obedience to the Word of God. It means we are choosing to be set free from living under the power of the offense any longer! If the offense happened twenty years ago and you are still harboring resentment, you are keeping it alive. If you forgive, you kill it right here, right now. Forgive and be set free.

Here are a few practical ways you can begin practicing forgiveness today:

1. Acknowledging the issue and seeing the benefits of forgiveness versus the cost of resentment

2. Spending time with God and asking him to help you forgive

3. Talking with a counselor or pastor about forgiveness

One way you can begin forgiving others today is through prayer, and when I pray, I like to follow the pattern Jesus used in the Lord's Prayer. Begin each day with recognizing God as your heavenly Father and then expressing gratitude for all he has done. Start with thanking him for his Son, Jesus, for the cross, for his resurrection, for his mercy and grace. Begin to thank him for everything and every person in your life. When you get to the part about forgiveness, spend a little extra time here. Maybe begin to forgive others in prayer with no expectation of any change in your own heart right away.

Here's one way I practice this: "I know I have a lot of things I need your forgiveness for, God, and I know there are going to be things today I need covered by your mercy. But I want to take a moment and forgive (insert name) for lying about me and (insert name) for hurting me, and I know you will forgive them as I have forgiven them. Please forgive me for all my sins, both known and unknown." You could even start on a simpler note and say, "I forgive those who have caused me harm, trouble, and grief, and I ask for you to forgive me for my sins too."

It's not necessarily a requirement that you communicate in any way with the individual or groups of people who have hurt you. In fact, unless it is a close family member or friend, even someone in your local church, it may be best to not approach them and let your forgiveness be between you and God. The reality is that choosing to forgive is an indicator of spiritual maturity, and the offender may not be ready to process this issue just yet.

However, there may be times when you need forgiveness from a spouse, family member, or friend. Having a healthy conversation with them about the matter can lead to forgiveness, but as a follower of Christ, consider leading with, "I was wrong when I (insert offense). Will you forgive me?" Notice I did not say apologize. There is a significant difference between apologizing and asking for forgiveness. We can apologize for what we did even though we aren't sorry for why we did it. It does not require humility like asking for forgiveness requires. Forgiveness leads to repentance, while apologizing leaves an open-ended opportunity for us to reoffend. Choose forgiveness every time.

Addressing forgiveness requires a conscious decision to do so, and we cannot do it flippantly. We must choose to forgive and willingly do so based on the condition of our spiritual being and not only by our intellectual decision-making abilities. While others who have hurt you may not accept personal responsibility for their actions and ask you for forgiveness, taking a step of faith and forgiving them while you are in pursuit of a closer walk with Jesus will lead to a better life. It will help you gain a better perspective of who God is as our Father and Savior. Who are we to refuse forgiveness when we have been so freely forgiven?

Knowing the benefits available, I hope you will join me in this, as it has been the single biggest factor in overcoming the trauma in my life. Not only because I chose to forgive but also because I discovered how much God loves to forgive my sins. It has been a game changer for my health, my spiritual maturity, and the discovery of my gifts. If we harbor resentments and hold on to grudges, it blocks answers to prayers and keeps us from walking in the gifts God has given us.

## Unconquered Code #4

Discover freedom in forgiveness. It's not for the offender; it's for you.

## Battle Action Step

Go into your bathroom or another room where there is a mirror and look into your eyes. Repeat these words: "I don't want to, but because Jesus told me to, I choose to forgive. I let go of all resentment and any grudges and choose to live in freedom from the offense."

## Discussion

1. What are some of the physical health benefits of forgiveness?

2. How did Jesus teach us to pray as it relates to forgiving one another?

3. Write a letter to the person who offended you and forgive them in the letter, then either destroy it or keep it in a safe place to remind yourself of this choice you made.

## Prayer

*Heavenly Father, I cannot carry the burden of pain and sin in my own strength any longer. I am asking you to forgive me of every sin in my life, those I am aware I have committed and those I am not aware I have committed. In the same way, I am coming to you today and opening my hands to forgive those who have hurt me. You know the details, and I am giving it all to you. Soften my heart toward you and heal the pain in my life. Thank you for your mercy and grace. Amen.*

*Everybody in the world is seeking happiness—*
*and there is one sure way to find it.*
*That is by controlling your thoughts.*
*Happiness doesn't depend on outward conditions.*
*It depends on inner conditions.*

DALE CARNEGIE[22]

## PRINCIPLE #5

# POLICE YOUR THOUGHTS

*[Cast] down arguments and every high thing that exalts itself against the knowledge of God, bringing every thought into captivity to the obedience of Christ.*

2 CORINTHIANS 10:5 NKJV

Violent crimes are increasing in most cities across the United States. In Los Angeles, California, alone, the homicide rate in 2021 was the highest in fifteen years. Look at many cities around the nation, and this number is trending upward. But, as with any criminal statistics, the only numbers we see are those cases reported, which means the number may not be an accurate representation of how much crime is actually occurring.

One of the most underreported crimes in the United States[23] and internationally is human trafficking, with more than 108,000 individual human-trafficking cases around the world reported in 2020 alone.[24] Statistics are an easy way for us to forget that each number represents a human life.

For every person who is working to lure in a victim, someone else is paying them. It costs money to conduct this level of criminal activity, and each victim represents a dollar value to the leadership of these organized crime rings. The methods for obtaining funding for these types of operations by criminal enterprises are often complex and unseen by the average American, and they often involve international ties.

During my assignment to the criminal investigations division, I primarily investigated commercial and residential burglaries. Most of my days in investigations were incredibly busy with mountains of paperwork, follow-up calls, and an occasional rush from executing warrants or pursuing a suspect. I also had a few violent crime cases along the way. Helping bring closure for victims of violent crimes is a sacred duty.

One of the most memorable cases I had the opportunity to participate in was a temporary detail with a federal law enforcement agency. Along with the agents I was assigned to work with, I conducted surveillance on a suspect who played a key role in a human trafficking operation. His primary objective was to secure finances for the furtherance of their criminal activity. Once we were finished obtaining the information we needed through surveillance, we approached the suspect and initiated a traffic stop. During our briefing, the senior federal agent had told me the suspect was well versed in martial arts and was likely armed and dangerous, so we had to move swiftly to safely bring him into custody.

We exited the unmarked vehicle, approached the driver's side of the suspect's vehicle, grabbed him, and put handcuffs on him immediately while simultaneously explaining to him who we were and what was going on. There was no room for error because he had stopped in the middle of the highway. It felt incredible to put in custody someone who had a hand in a major human trafficking ring, but my heart was thumping so hard I could hear it in my ears. There's no doubt I had an adrenaline rush from that apprehension.

As the hours passed during the interrogation of the suspect, I listened to him share the details of how he and his criminal enterprise obtained funds and their heartless, evil views of human beings as nothing more than a product. Because it was a federal crime and I was not with the lead agency, I was not responsible for the interrogation. However, I was able to learn a lot by observing. It really wouldn't have mattered if I had been a law enforcement officer or not. Those details would have brought about rage in the mind of any reasonable human being.

If you're not careful, those same negative emotions and thoughts can cause you to become blind to the truth you are in pursuit of. When you're not on your A game, suspects can walk away free, the giants you are called to slay become your masters, and you can surrender to temptations in your life. There's always a consequence for not controlling your emotions, and those negative thoughts are the engine behind them.

Whether I was on patrol or interrogating a suspect in the criminal investigations division, maintaining composure and controlling emotions and thoughts were essential for living victoriously. And while I was good at handling them at work, I had tremendous room for improvement in dealing with them at home.

### The Universal Issue That Can Lead to Defeat

For most of my life, toxic and negative thoughts have been a burden. Now, if you would have asked me if I experienced fear, I'd tell you I wasn't afraid of anything, but the reality was that my ego was speaking for me. It was pride. Worry, anxiety, stress, and doubt had a grip on me and were consuming my life. I began having terrible panic attacks, becoming physically ill, and snapping at those I loved dearly.

About seven years ago, I realized my issue wasn't necessarily externally sourced. Rather, it was my mindset and thought patterns. It was life-changing for me when I learned that I could change my thought patterns. It took a while for me to learn the enemy of our souls cannot read our minds, but he knows the patterns, and he attacks that rhythm.

There's a dangerous enemy who wants to kill you, but there's a more dangerous God who isn't afraid to do battle on your behalf. All we have to do is call on him and ask for his help. In every situation where we are facing negative emotions, we have a choice. We can allow those negative emotions to dominate our lives, or we can overwhelm them with the force of truth. Sometimes we just need to be still in the presence of the living God and, by his power, slap the spiritual and mental handcuffs on those lying, negative thoughts and judge them by the standard of God's Word.

While we all have negative thought patterns, we can change them by following Scripture and developing healthy daily habits. A negative mindset is that which bears no fruit and is contrary to the truth of God's Word. It's the Philippians 4:8 rule: "Finally, brothers and sisters, whatever is true, whatever is noble, whatever is right, whatever is pure, whatever is lovely, whatever is admirable—if anything is excellent or praiseworthy—think about such things" (NIV). This is the standard for judging our thoughts. Our mindset battles are won at the point of resistance. We say we feel defeated because that is the dominant thought pattern, but God calls us more than a conqueror. Our thoughts do not align with the truth. We wallow in worry when Jesus tells us not to worry numerous times throughout the New Testament. We surrender to temptation when he says he has provided a way out. It's always at the point of friction and resistance where we make the decision to exchange the unholy thoughts for the thoughts he says are good and excellent.

When you decide to attack negative thinking, you will most assuredly experience resistance from your old ways of thinking. It will be challenging to overcome these issues because you have likely grown accustomed to this way of living for many years, but it's only challenging if you are unaware of the standard and how to flip those thoughts. Once you have the tools and the standard by which to gauge those things, you can begin to make the necessary changes in your daily life to shift the patterns. Yes, it requires effort, and it's going to take time and consistency, but laziness never developed anything good. I do know our thinking habits tend to create the outcomes we have in life.

## Changing of the Guard

As a child, I was required to attend church frequently; it was not an option nor a suggestion. Oftentimes when I am speaking at an event, I jokingly say we were in church twelve days a week. Someone once came up to me after an event and said, "You know there are only seven days in a week, right?" I chuckled and clarified what I meant: we were in church every time the doors were open and sometimes when they weren't open to the public! In fact, I attended so much, they let me become a member, and I remember signing the church membership card that required me to agree to no dancing, no music except Christian music, no movies, and other restrictions that seemed so asinine. I vividly recall having a "secular CD burning party" with the youth group at church on several occasions. Rest in peace to those Hank Williams Jr. CDs.

In my young and ignorant teenage mind, all these things were way too strict. Even today, I think dancing is a good thing if you have the moves! Seriously, there's no way we can live our lives by some unattainable standard. However, I do believe there is some degree of validity to being cautious of what you allow in your mind through your eyes and ears, whether through movies, television, social media, music, books, or gossip. It only takes a second to allow things into your mind that can wreak havoc for a long time, and it takes a lot of discipline to get those things cleared out and cleaned up.

How do we differentiate between what we should enter-tain and what we must arrest? God established the standard in Philippians 4:8, and we must address anything contrary to it. Our minds are full of thoughts that have blossomed from the seeds planted by content in television, movies, music, video games, books, and every other medium that delivers content through our eyes and ears. And just like those nega-tive thoughts can blossom, there are godly thoughts that can blossom into beautiful harvests if we will be intentional with what we allow into our minds.

A 2005 article by the National Science Foundation gave an overview of research regarding the daily number of thoughts a person has. The article indicated that the aver-age person has between twelve thousand and sixty thousand thoughts each day. Additionally, 80 percent of those thoughts were considered negative, whereas 95 percent were identical thoughts as the previous day.[25]

Now, there are 1,440 minutes in a day, no matter how rich you are, what your occupation is, or where you live. We all get the same allotment of minutes each day while we are alive. If we take the lower end of that range of thoughts per day, say twelve thousand, that means every minute we are alive, we are having more than eight thoughts per minute. And if the study proves accurate, roughly seven of those eight thoughts are negative, and more than seven and a half are the exact same thoughts as the day before. We're stuck on repeat, on autopilot, and most of it is negative.

If we look at the upper range of the number of thoughts a person has per day at sixty thousand, that equates to more than forty-one thoughts per minute! Our minds are incredibly busy, and only a small fraction of those thoughts is positive or beneficial to us. This is a critical issue to address because our thoughts are based on our belief system, our val-ues, and they determine the words we speak, our behavior, and our actions. They dictate what habits control us and ultimately steer our lives.

If you think about how negative thoughts, depression, and anxiety have increased over time, it's also important to consider the advancement of technology over time. Never before have we had more influences and sources feeding us thoughts. Seventy years ago the sources of reporting were limited to television, newspapers, and some magazines. Televisions weren't in every home although they were becoming more popular. Since the arrival of smartphones, smartwatches, and social media platforms, we are consumers of news media 24/7. Around the clock and every day of the year, we receive sources of violence, mayhem, panic, fear, and all the other negative seeds of thought you can imagine. Never have we had more access to more news and real-time violence than now.

Controlling negative thoughts must have been easier seventy years ago, with less influence and fewer sources to feed them. We are receiving bad news at our fingertips and checking for that news like it's a drug. On top of the 24/7 news feed of toxic information being fed into our minds like an IV, we're taking our phones to bed. We stay up into the wee hours to get our next fix of social media, entertainment, and bad news. We can't get enough! Our sleep is not healthy, our minds are not getting rested and restored, and the cycle continues. No wonder evil is rampant.

The good news is we have been deputized by the authority in heaven, the high sheriff, because of his Son, Jesus, and we are equipped and empowered, fully authorized to take into custody every thought that does not align with his Word. Most of the time, when we are facing a challenge or obstacle in life, the number one enemy we must deal with first is ourselves. We get in the way of our own success.

I know it is a bit presumptuous, but I believe most people, especially law enforcement and other first responders, know the challenges they face every day against their emotions, mind, body, and well-being. The universal issues that span every career, line of work, ethnicity, and nationality are our emotions and thoughts. It's not a matter of how much money you have or don't have or your relationship status. We all have emotions, and we all have thoughts. To experience victory in life, we must learn to master them both.

I allowed past events of my life to con me into believing I had to repeat those events or even relive them in my mind, my emotions, and my life. I believed it was a life sentence. I like to think it was something I was taught early in my childhood, but there is a great deal I have discovered about worry as I have aged. Most of the things I worried about never happened. All it did was rob me of the joy I could have experienced at the moment I was worrying. It is not situational. You can have $2 in the bank and $100,000 in debt, or you can have $10 million in the bank and no debt, but if you do not address the root of worry in your mind, you will still have the issue no matter what.

While I am cautious when it comes to some who suggest we can "name it and claim it" when seeking things in life, I do believe that God's Word is true and infallible. Therefore, everything we do in life stems from what is in our minds and inner will. Those thoughts we entertain, the same 95 percent from yesterday and the day before, are either leading you down a road to victory or are the root cause of the constant onslaught of battles in your life. Proverbs 4:23 reads, "Above all else, guard your heart, for everything you do flows from it" (NIV).

A sidenote and intersecting fact here. In the Old Testament, the writer of Proverbs wrote using the Hebrew language in the original manuscript. When looking at the original writing, the word *heart* specifically refers to the inner will, or the mind, of a person.[26] I'm not suggesting we can use our minds to create physical things from nothing because everything that was created in Genesis was created by God, the Creator of all things. However, I do believe Proverbs 4:23 is clear in that our minds have tremendous power to generate good or evil in our lives. After all, it says "everything you do flows from it" (your mind, your inner will).

Thus the case is made that our minds, our thoughts, and our will play an important role in whether we will live a victorious life or a defeated life. Most people who profess to be followers of Christ fall short of understanding the true power they possess through the relationship God provided by sending his Son, Jesus, for our redemption.

Allow me to pose this question: Who watches your thoughts? Better yet, who *guards* your heart, or your mind and inner will? Is it you? How do you do that? We cannot see our thoughts, nor can we see our minds or inner will. I suggest it is the Holy Spirit who guards our hearts and minds, only if we relinquish control and authority to him to do so. Jesus said it was necessary for him to go so he could send the Holy Spirit, our Comforter. When we choose to wallow in our own thoughts, when we choose to entertain negative thoughts and the lies we've been programmed to believe, we fall short of knowing who we are in Christ. What tragedy life is when we fail to live it to the fullest because we do not have the full knowledge of who he is and what we have access to through Jesus.

There's only one way to remedy our thoughts, and that is to bring them into alignment with the truth of God's Word. What does he say about you? What does he say about worry, fear, or the future? While I don't know every detail about every situation in your life, God knows. He knows everything. He knows our hurt, our pain, and he knows the memories we cannot shake. Every thought we have, he knows. It is only by knowing the truth about life, pain, death, loss, and suffering that we can live forward in power and victory. That's the only way we can live unconquered.

When we choose to buy the lies of the enemy with every thought, we choose to miss out on living life to the fullest. This isn't about making more money, getting new cars or houses, or landing that dream job. Although those things are good and possible, the goal is to get out of our own heads and eliminate the negative thought loops so we can discover who we are in Christ and what he says about us.

One of the biggest strengths I possess today comes from having to survive trauma and pain as a child. I learned how to survive through unspeakable pain as a young boy. I knew manipulation and deception as a teenager, on a very real level, and I spent most of my life surviving while wanting to die.

Now that I can look back at all those events and recall some memories, I believe my desire to end my life was really just a place of total and complete exhaustion. I no longer had the capacity to continue with the weight of the burdens I carried, and I felt helpless. But while I learned an uncommon strength very young, I also learned to hide and suppress pain and compartmentalize in an unhealthy way.

## The Beauty of Our Minds

God is the ultimate Creator, and when he created us, he created our minds to be incredibly complex and powerful. Because I am not able to comprehend every moving part of the brain or digest the massive amount of information on the subject, I will touch briefly on two parts of the mind: the conscious and the subconscious mind.

Think about the mind like an iceberg. You see a little tip out of the water, but underneath is a massive mountain of ice exponentially larger than what is visible. The part we can "see" is our conscious mind, and underneath it, working around the clock, is our subconscious mind.

Another way to look at these parts of our mind is to think about a computer monitor. When you see the images and content on a screen, you do not see the millions of lines of code and all the processes going on behind the scenes. We can liken the screen to our consciousness. It is what we are aware of. The power behind the scenes operating that computer is the subconscious mind. That's the part of your mind that is helping process this information, but there's so much more to it.

Those seeds that modern technology has planted in our minds through unending news feeds blossom into aggravating and fast-growing weeds in what is a beautiful garden of a mind. It's supposed to be fruitful, flourishing, and productive. But if we don't deal with the origin of these issues, fear, worry, and feelings that we aren't good enough or even lovable will continue to sprout up. It's like trying to mow down weeds in your lawn but being surprised when they sprout back up a day later. You have to remove them, root and all. It took me a long time to figure this out. You can't see how beautiful the garden is because the weeds have taken over. Satan can't read your mind, but he can influence what you dwell on by presenting you with things that will appeal to your carnal nature. Resist those things and cling to the truth of God's Word.

Let's get equipped for the battle to police our thoughts by breaking down Philippians 4:8. Here is this verse from a different translation:

> Finally, brethren, whatever things are true, whatever things are noble, whatever things are just, whatever things are pure, whatever things are lovely, whatever things are of good report, if there is any virtue and if there is anything praiseworthy—meditate on these things. (NKJV)

Here is the standard by which we are to judge our thoughts:

- What is true? Truth is what we find in God as we read in 2 Timothy 2:25, what is found in Jesus in Ephesians 4:20–21, in the Holy Spirit in John 16:13, and in the Bible in John 17:17. Measure up information as either a lie or truth against this standard.
- What is noble? Philippians was written originally in Greek. Looking at the word *noble* in the Greek, the term means "worthy of respect." We are to dwell on whatever is worthy of awe and adoration, resist the profane, and embrace the holy.
- What is just? Dwell on that which is right. Our thoughts should be in harmony with God's divine standard of holiness, not man's attempt to redefine it.
- What is pure? Pure is morally clean and undefiled.
- What is lovely? The Greek term means "pleasing" or "amiable." We are to focus on whatever is kind or gracious.
- What is of good report? It refers to that which is highly regarded and what is generally considered reputable in the world, such as kindness, courtesy, and respect for others.[27]
- What is excellent or praiseworthy? This means it is good or worth talking about. We do not need to dwell on everything.

Addressing these issues, especially if you have lived with a negative mindset and negative thoughts for a long time, will take some effort. However, if you are willing to approach the throne room of God and seek his help, he will provide you with the insight and understanding to attack this issue and experience victory. This is one of the most critical keys to live unconquered: fix your mindset and police your thoughts.

## God Can Use for Our Good What the Enemy Meant for Evil

In my time as a negotiator, we had several "live negotiations," which means they were real, active negotiations, not training scenarios. One was with a man who took his significant other hostage and had a firearm pointed at her head. His goal was for her to witness him take his life. There were several similar situations, but we never lost anyone. The case that stands out in my mind the most was a hostage situation that lasted about a week. Since this story was covered in *The Wall Street Journal* and almost every other major news outlet, most of the details are common knowledge.

The suspect, Jimmy Lee Dykes, boarded a school bus full of children and demanded the bus driver release one child to him.[28] Dykes was not the guardian, parent, or caregiver, but he had a firearm. "I don't want to shoot you," Dykes told the bus driver, Chuck Poland. Dykes had been preparing for this moment. He had hired someone to help him dig an underground bunker, fully prepared for a long-term stay. When Poland, a beloved member of the community in Dale County, Alabama, refused to give in to Dykes' demand, he was murdered in front of a school bus full of children. Then, Dykes grabbed the first child within his reach, a five-year-old boy named Ethan, and he took him into his underground bunker.

It wasn't long before every media outlet across the country was present, as well as the FBI and a number of other agencies. In negotiations, typically a primary negotiator and a secondary negotiator work along with other support team members. For much of my time on the scene, I was a secondary negotiator.

SWAT team members deployed a phone into the bunker for Dykes to communicate his "demands" with law enforcement. As I sat in the command center monitoring video and audio of Dykes and Ethan, I found myself seeing the little five-year-old boy as one of my own children since, at the time of the incident, one of my children was around the same age. It broke my heart as I listened to the suspect talk to the child like a dog at times, not to mention forcing him to live in an underground bunker with his ultimate plan of killing the boy and a lot of other people.

Somewhere about halfway through the hostage situation, my superiors and hostage negotiations team commander pulled me from the scene for a discussion. They were concerned that I had become too emotionally attached to the boy to make clear decisions. What they didn't know is every night or early morning after I would get home, I would wake my kids up and hold them. Maybe I had become too close to the boy, to the case. Maybe I saw him as the five-year-old version of myself. In the end, the suspect was killed, the boy was rescued, and the bus driver, Mr. Poland, will forever be remembered for the lives he saved, the life he lived, and the impact he had on a small Alabama community.

I had not been the dad my children needed or that I longed to be in my heart until this case. In fact, it was one of the cases that had the greatest impact on me because it made me see just how precious children are, especially my own. It caused me to shift my thoughts from being a selfish person and try to focus on being a better dad, being more intentional about attending their events, and building a better life for them to give them the best opportunity for life.

Sometimes the battles that come our way test our resolve, thinking, and mindset, and in some cases, they make us stronger. That's resiliency. Because of my battles and pain, I am stronger. Had it not been for the standard of God's Word and what he says wholesome thinking is, I'm not sure where I'd be today. His Word is a lamp that lights our path. Let it shine into the darkness that has overwhelmed your mind and show you the best way to live with an unconquered mindset.

## The Mindset Makeover Checklist

*Decide to Take Action*

We must decide in our hearts and minds that we are going to do something about our negative mindset.

*Do They Meet the Standard?*

If our mindset doesn't meet the standard set forth in Philippians 4:8 of thoughts that are true, noble, right, pure, lovely, admirable, excellent, or praiseworthy, those thoughts must be addressed and changed. We can only do this through reading and studying God's Word and through a relationship with Jesus.

*Clean Out the Closet*

Literally cleaning out closets has a positive psychological effect. Cleaning out our inner closets does the same. What are you harboring? What negative emotions do you hold on to? Why? Let the negative go, forgive those who wronged you, and begin healing.

*Create a Prayer Strategy*

Having a strategy will help you become more organized in your efforts. Here's a helpful start:

- Pray for the Holy Spirit to help you police your thoughts.
- Pray for the strength to remain resilient in this battle.
- Pray for your heart and mind to be drawn to the things of God.
- Pray for a softened heart.
- Pray against the temptations of this world.
- Pray for the ability to see the world through God's eyes.

### Have a Daily Routine

What is your current daily routine? Morning routine? Evening? Take time to look at your current habits and patterns. What are the areas you want to change? What are areas you need to change?

### Get Healthy

Being physically active helps you to keep your brain healthy and become more aware of the thoughts you are entertaining. Whether it is monitoring your daily steps or working out in the gym for at least thirty minutes a day, doing something is better than doing nothing.

### Hire a Coach, Find a Mentor

Having someone invest in your life is invaluable. Having someone who has already been down the road you are planning to travel will save you time, heartache, and money.

## Unconquered Code #5

Take captive your emotions and align them with the truth of God's Word.

## Battle Action Step

Identify harmful, unhealthy thinking habits, patterns, and the sources of them. Begin putting the Mindset Makeover Challenge to work in your life today.

## Discussion

1. What are some of the sources that feed negative thinking in your life?

2. How do you see negative thoughts wreaking havoc in different areas of your life?

3.  Write down Philippians 4:8 on a notepad or set a reminder on your phone to go off every few hours to remind you to properly align your thinking.

## Prayer

*Heavenly Father, I recognize that some of my thoughts do not align with the standard set forth in your Word. And I acknowledge that I have entertained thoughts that are not in line with Philippians 4:8. I am asking you to give me the strength, willpower, and wisdom to address these with the strategies provided. Thank you for your Word, and thank you for a better way of thinking. As I read your Word, renew my mind. Amen.*

*Growing closer to God
is not the result of trying harder
but of surrendering more.*

Anonymous

## PRINCIPLE #6

# THE SIGNIFICANCE OF SURRENDER

*Submit yourselves, then, to God.*
*Resist the devil, and he will flee from you.*

JAMES 4:7 NIV

It was Father's Day 2019, and my wife and kids whisked me away to the beautiful beaches along the Florida Gulf Coast. To this day, it still feels like a dream come true that I am their father. It's one of the wildest adventures and most rewarding things in life. Once we arrived at the beach, we decided to start the day off by getting an early lunch from a locally owned and family-operated restaurant then head to the beach for a few hours.

Sometime that afternoon, I suppose around early to midafternoon, I took a black tube to float on and waded into the gulf about waist deep. Before I could get into the tube and relax, I noticed something out of the ordinary. At approximately my eleven o'clock, about twenty to thirty yards out or so, I noticed a woman's head bobbing up and down in the water before disappearing underneath the surface again. Her face was not that of someone relaxing in the water; she was obviously in distress.

I began kicking my legs and using my arms as hard as I could to get to the lady so I could render aid, but another man came to her within a few seconds. Before too long, they were both in distress. They had no way of getting to shore, but I wasn't sure why they were both in trouble. Was there a shark? That was my first thought, sadly. I had no way of knowing at the moment.

Once I made my way to the man and woman, whom I later found out were married and from Louisiana, I gave them my tube, and they kicked their way back into the shore. But before I could make my way to the shore behind them, the water began pulling me farther out.

I don't know how far out I was pulled, but I recall looking up in an instant and seeing my wife and kids standing on the beach looking for me and waving their hands. I noticed they looked really small. I was fighting with all my strength, but the more I fought, the farther out I was pulled. It was unlike anything I'd ever experienced in my life. I had no control, and the more I fought to get out, the worse it got.

Something in my brain clicked. I'm not sure if it was the public service announcements regarding rip currents and how to get out of one if you found yourself being pulled away or if it was something else. The thought hit me: be still. Go with the flow of the water. So I quit thrashing my arms and legs and trying to swim against the current, relaxed, and drifted parallel to the beach with the waves. It wasn't too long after this that I was able to walk onshore, where my wife and kids greeted me.

What I saw next quickly shifted my mood as there were a number of people who were standing on the beach with smartphones in hand, camera lens pointed to the ocean and looking at me. They had been recording me in my struggle, and it made me incredibly angry. I thought, *Why in the world would you stand there and not come help me?* I embraced my wife and kids, and the couple I had given my float to came over and told me it was the first time in their twenty-five years visiting the beach that this had ever happened. We talked for a few minutes and parted ways. It was a memorable Father's Day but one that could have quickly turned into a very bad day.

After that experience at the beach, I began to think about some of the different situations I have dealt with in life and how we deal with the push and pull of different parts of our lives. For what seemed to be several minutes, I couldn't catch my breath while being taken captive by the ocean. I couldn't fight against the mass of water, no matter how strong I thought I was. I think about that day and consider the possibility of my family watching me get swept out into the ocean to die, and I wonder what it might mean if we live a life of surrender. Instead of thrashing against the battles in life, surrender to the one who called us more than a conqueror because he knows who we are in him.

## It's Counterintuitive

If something is pulling you underwater, your initial reaction is to fight, resist, and get as far away as possible from whatever "it" is. But if that something is a rip current, you aren't supposed to fight against it. If that's not counterintuitive, I don't know what is. I came home that day with my family, and later that week, I told a friend of mine about what had happened in the water. He jokingly said, "You don't have a lot of good luck with water, do you?" He was right. There have been several battles in my life involving water, and this was just one. Previously I had shared about a trip where the boat I was on began sinking in a storm and a separate story where alligators surrounded us in a slew when the boat's engine wouldn't start.

Don't get me wrong, I'm not suggesting you surrender to every battle you face in life; just surrender to God. That's it. If you're battling cancer, fight like hell. If you're battling depression, don't give up. If you're fighting to overcome an addiction, know there are people who are waiting to fight alongside you. There's no one-size-fits-all guide for every battle in life, but there is a one-size-fits-all approach to salvation, and that's through Jesus.

There have been many battles I have struggled with in life, and you know, in the end, I learned a lot from those experiences. As I thought about what really matters in life, it all boiled down to serving God, loving my family well, and loving others. Finding the point of surrender seldom comes easily, and it is often discovered in the heat of battle, just when you are ready to walk away from the fight. Instead of quitting, surrender. That's the key. And there will be times when you may still lose your way, even when you think you have it all together and figured out. Live each day like it is your last because you could leave this life today. Surrender often.

## Trust and Surrender

I am often asked, "Why did you become a law enforcement officer?" As I shared in an earlier chapter, my dad has owned a small business in our hometown for over four decades, and it was not out of the norm in his line of work to meet law enforcement officers regularly. We towed vehicles involved in motor vehicle collisions, and Dad and his crew repaired them. I grew up learning what it meant to work hard, and I saw how much work law enforcement officers put in. I saw how they interacted with others, and when our families got together, their families made a positive impression on me.

I wanted *my* family to be like that, and I wanted to be like those men when I grew up. They became sort of like heroes to me, I guess. So, I became a cop. While "to help others" seems like a cliché answer to "Why did you become a cop?," it was the most straightforward answer I could provide every time someone asked that question of me.

The reality is that I became a police officer because of the men and women in law enforcement whom I saw as a teenager. It was still about serving, protecting, and helping others, but it was also about becoming someone my family would be proud to call their own. I wanted to make my family proud, and I wanted to serve my city with pride and honor.

You see, I became a good cop because the best cops surrounded me. They were the best of the best, in training and on the streets. To this very day, I believe the men and women I served with were among the best of the best in our nation. But I didn't become a law enforcement officer, an effective cop, or even decent at my job on my own.

The seventeenth-century author John Donne once wrote a sermon, and one of the lines from his sermon says, "No man is an island."[29] If I were to get a tattoo on my body, that quote would be it. Why? Because no cop is self-made, and you better not get caught trying to be a cowboy cop or lone ranger. We relied on each other. We trusted each other because we had to rely on each other. That often makes me wonder that, if that was such a strong desire of mine to be a family man, a good husband, and father and to serve my community with honor and pride, then why did I let the evil of this world harden my heart? It nearly destroyed me, my marriage, and the call on my life to serve.

Maybe the secret in this entire book about living victoriously is found right here, in this chapter. A principle that is so countercultural and counterintuitive that it sends shockwaves through an evil and wicked society. This is the secret for living unconquered and the superpower of people you have watched come out of the fires of life with the embers of hell still clinging to their clothes. They weren't affected by the fire. In fact, they turned around and went back to get one more person out of the fires of life.

What will you do? Will you choose to walk in your own power, in your own strength, or will you opt to live in the way of the supernatural? That is, surrendered wholeheartedly to God.

## When the Fight Gets the Best of You

Most of my life has been a lesson in surrender, and while I am approaching the halfway point in this life, I believe I am just beginning to grasp this concept. What does it look like to be someone who refuses to give up the pain, the burdens, the weight of life? It looks like the way of the world. The world teaches us that we never surrender, and while that is a proper mindset for an earthly battle, it is the opposite for the kingdom of God.

Quick rabbit trail here: the kingdom of God is mostly opposite of everything you see here in this world. The world says if you want to be first and be exalted, you go for what you want and take it. But if you want to be first in God's kingdom, you surrender, submit to him, and he will exalt you. God's Word says to seek first his kingdom, and all the other things you want and long for will be added. It's contrary to the way of the world. So if you've been carrying stuff around in your heart or head for decades, there's no condemnation; it's all you've known to do. But now, you will be introduced to a better way.

When I met Amber in high school, we became best friends. There was almost an immediate connection between us, and we couldn't stop talking. No matter the topic, we would talk until the teacher said to be quiet or, if it were late at night, until one of us fell asleep on the phone. I want you to grasp this point. We were, and I believe still are, best friends. Aside from Jesus, nobody else knows me as she does, and she still loves me. There's nothing I would not do for my wife and kids, but something happened after I became a law enforcement officer.

I'm not sure when I shut down or quit communicating with her as my best friend, but I remember one day after I finished a twelve-hour shift, I came home and removed my duty shirt, vest, and duty belt. I sat down in the living room and faced the television, staring at a blank screen. Behind me, I could hear the water running in the kitchen sink and Amber's voice as she asked, "How was your day?"

There was no response from me. I was a hull, an empty shell, completely tattered inside. Once again, she asked, "Babe, how was your day?" She didn't nag, although in the moment, that's what I thought she was doing.

Finally, I mustered up the energy to respond with, "It was fine." I didn't want to relive the day. It was bad enough to go through it once, much less a second time by discussing it.

She responded, "Adam, when did you become such a jerk? I'm trying to talk to you, I've made dinner and been nothing but nice, and you just sit there and stare at the wall. What's your deal?"

I was so full of pride, so selfish, so numb to any resemblance of emotion or consciousness that I was ready to end everything. She didn't know that. She just saw that her best friend was physically present but otherwise missing from the marriage.

"I'm fine," I replied curtly. "Please, just let me be. I don't want to relive today. It took everything I had to make it home, and I'd like to forget about it, please."

When did I quit showing up for my marriage? When I put everything else before her. I lost my will to work on myself and our marriage and took her for granted. I stayed quiet, grabbed a few things, and left. All that was a blur, and I don't remember what else was said, but I know it wasn't love. It was Adam looking out for Adam. That's it. And that's not what marriage is about. It's about looking out for each other, fighting like hell for what matters most.

That night and the following nights I stayed in a small office building adjacent to one of my dad's shops.

"Son, you can come to stay at the house. I have a room for you," he said.

I didn't want to be a burden anymore. I took the bait from hell—hook, line, and sinker—that I was a burden to my wife and kids, my other family members, the department, and everyone else in my life. If you feel like a liability and burden to everyone, the "they'd be better off if I were dead" thoughts seem to bear more weight.

Night after night, I would seclude myself in this small shack, wishing, hoping, praying for an answer from within. But there was nothing. Just one raging battle in my soul. I buried myself in work, taking as many off-duty hours as I could get, working any time I had free. I'd say it was for the money, and that was partly true, but the fact was, I was trying to find a way to carry this all in my own strength and ability. For months it was a fifteen-round heavyweight bout between me and God, or so I thought.

My pride and desire for self-sufficiency had led me to a place where I was essentially interrogating God. "You say you're good, but what about these children who are being maimed? What about the innocent?" I'd say to him. "You say you're love, but what about…" and on and on I went.

I still cringe when I think about who I was then because how incredibly stupid and arrogant do you have to be to think you can interrogate God? In the midst of it all, he never stopped loving me. I dare suggest that if you have questions for God, he is big enough to handle them, just be sure you approach them with the right heart. His grace is sufficient for all our needs. Even when we are lost and hurting, his grace covers us when we are stupid enough to think we're interrogating him.

As the days passed, I continued to seek answers. I continued to interrogate God—not about his existence but rather about his goodness and love. All the while, both his goodness and love were evident in so many parts of my life. He was with me through it all.

## Victory in Surrender

It had crossed my mind on more than one occasion that maybe, just maybe, my family, friends, and everyone else would have been better off had I never been born. I knew they'd miss my physical presence for a bit and be sad, but in the end, they'd be better off. No more moody Adam, no more mess, just peace with his storm. In my eyes, everything I touched turned into a big mess: my marriage, work, family, you name it. I was a wreck.

Suicide had crossed my mind for a long time, primarily due to the pain I experienced as a child, teenager, and adult. It seemed that I was created to experience pain and defeat. But for what purpose? How do you respond when abuse is swept under the rug by people you trusted with every fiber of your being, only for them to declare their support for pedophiles and blame you as a five-year-old victim?

There I was: separated from my wife and children. I had shunned and pushed away from me the very core of who I was as a man, everything I wanted to become. I sat in my patrol car in an abandoned parking lot, something I had done many times before, either working on a report or watching for traffic violations, but this day was different. My marriage had taken a turn for the worse, and things had gotten really bad.

I had come to terms with my own mortality, that I would absolutely, without a doubt, die. Attending the funerals of law enforcement officers jolted me. Not to mention having seen things I wasn't prepared to see as a cop: the mangled bodies, headshot wounds, suicides, children and women raped, murders, you name it. Maybe it made me weak; maybe it made me human. For me, what happened in the patrol car wasn't a result of one situation; it was everything piling up on me, building and building until it became too much to carry.

As I held my service weapon in my left hand, resting it on top of my left thigh, tears ran down my face; this was it. There would soon be no more pain, no more failure, no more rejection. My heart raced, beating so fast, so hard, that I could feel it in my fingertips. All the emotions you could fathom were present. It was a reality check.

Then, it was just stillness. Quiet. Everything faded around me. I mustered up one last breath in all my seeming brokenness and said to God, "I don't know if you can hear me. I don't even know where you're at, but I've made a mess of my life, and if you can do anything with it, you can have it. But if you can't, I am taking it."

I was tired. I was beaten down. I felt defeated.

My life didn't end in that patrol car, and suicide wasn't the end of my story. Pain wasn't the end of my story. I would later see that this moment was just the beginning. All because of surrender.

In the instant I cried out to God in utter imperfection and wretchedness, he met me. Right there, in a marked patrol car. To this day I am thankful no one stopped to ask for directions or needed aid. It was definitely my God moment.

In the instant I called on him, I felt an embrace. But how could it be? I was alone. No one else was with me in the car or near me. In an instant, I experienced a perfect love, one I cannot explain or describe but one that became the leading force in my life. From that day forward, it became my life's mission—through writing, speaking, relationship building, whatever and however possible—to help as many people as I could to experience the love I felt in that moment. This was my new beginning.

## Perpetual Victory in Surrender

After my experience in that patrol car with God, everything in my life wasn't made perfect in an instant. There were still challenges along the way and things I needed to reconcile. The primary thing I needed to reconcile was my marriage.

Once I finished my shift, I went and found Amber and told her what happened, and God began to work on both of us. As I write about this, it still brings tears to my eyes thinking about just how good he has been to me and my family and his mercy and grace that saved me. But surrender isn't a one-time deal. It's not something that's over with when we walk to an altar and say a prayer in a church service while beautiful music plays. It's daily. And there are going to be moments in your life, pivotal moments, when your decision to surrender will mean either breakthrough or staying in the same spot in life. It's a lesson I am still learning.

After my encounter with God in the patrol car, I'd quit drinking alcohol every night, so I needed to replace that time with something else. So I began writing. It became a way for me to cope with some stuff I had rolling around in my head, and it was a way to help heal my soul from some invisible wounds.

One evening a few weeks later, I finished my patrol shift, went home, took off my gear, unstrapped the Velcro so I could remove my bulletproof vest, and sat down at my computer. As I began to write, I stopped and prayed. During my prayer, I sensed desperation and frustration, and I remember asking God, "Who is going to help us? Who will speak life into my brothers and sisters? Who will encourage them while it seems the world around us wants to destroy us?"

So, I began to write, and I felt compelled to write a devotional for law enforcement. Yet I wrestled with the idea. I wrestled with it because I felt unqualified. But I did it because I felt the need to encourage my fellow officers and myself. I did it because I recognized a gap. Although I know

I lacked the seminary training, professional writing experience, and a lifetime of law enforcement experience, I did it. I wrote the devotional, and then I self-published it.

As I sat down to write that evening and asked God who would speak life to law enforcement, I didn't have a plan—or desire—to write a book. I didn't expect to have him call me to do something. Writing a book was never a dream or goal of mine. Before going to God with a complaint, be sure you are ready for how he may respond. He may let you know you are the one he created to do something for him. It wasn't but a few short years later that my friends at BroadStreet Publishing gave me an opportunity to write and publish *Behind the Badge: 365 Daily Devotions for Law Enforcement.* To date, it has touched tens of thousands of law enforcement officers across the country. With every message, review, testimonial, every time a law enforcement officer shares how these devotionals have helped him or her, it is a reminder that, through surrender, we find victory. It's not just my victory, it's yours, and yours is for someone else. We win together.

## Your Lifetime of Victory Begins Here

Something is programmed within our minds that causes us to say, "I'm fine, I'm good" or "I can handle this on my own" when we face something tough in life. That is pride. And when we look for something to support the position of the significance of surrender, James 4:7–10 are the key verses that will lead us into a life of power and victory. It's only through submitting to God that we find victory over whatever giants we face, and when we opt to fight them in our own power, it's game over.

James 4:7 says, "Submit yourselves, then, to God. Resist the devil, and he will flee from you" (NIV). Submitting our lives to God means looking to him and saying, "I can't do this in my own power anymore. Please help!" Then, get out of his way. Stop the fighting in your own power and let him become the force that pulls you to safety. It doesn't stop there.

To defeat pride, which is the center of our carnal desire for self-sufficiency, we must not only submit our lives fully to him, but we must also seek to purify our hearts and cleanse our spirits. Look at the priests in the Old Testament. Before they could enter the tabernacle and minister to God, they were required to wash their hands in the bronze basin as a sign of spiritual cleansing. This is the place where we experience purification. It means we go to him in prayer and ask God to direct our lives, to keep us from temptation, and to deliver us from any source of evil in this world. This is found in James 4:8.

The next step is not nearly as popular as it should be today, but it is truth, and truth, no matter how unpopular, is still truth. James 4:9 says to grieve and wail. It means to repent. Turn around. If you're going north, go south. If you're running into a building that is on fire and about to explode, pivot 180 degrees and run the other way. It means instead of catering to an appetite for sin, we not only whisper a short prayer of salvation, but we also give our appetite for life to God, the one who created us. We develop a taste for the things of God instead of the things of this world.

Today, it may be a fight to find joy and meaning, or maybe it's a battle to find your purpose. You have likely discovered that the more you thrash trying to find it, the more confused you get. I don't know what is pulling you under and farther from your family and friends, isolating you into an abyss of pain and misery, but I do know that if you will stop fighting and let God pull you back, you will win. The significance of surrender is this: it is the point of your victory. Surrender to God and let him take on your burdens and lead you.

As I navigated through these battles I have shared, I began to journal, and I wanted to share with you some of the battle strategies for prayer God provided to me through each victory:

1.  Not every prayer needs to be a long prayer for God to hear it. God hears the whispers of "911" emergency prayers. He hears our mundane prayers too.

2.  There is a place of prayer we can live in, where we can pray continuously (see 1 Thessalonians 5:17), and it is possible through the Holy Spirit.

3.  Pray the Scriptures from God's Word over specific needs when you know them.

4.  Always begin prayer with thanksgiving and praise to God for who he is.

5.  Thank God for the cross.

6.  Thank God for the blood of his Son, Jesus.

7.  Recognize your need for cleansing by the sacrifice of Jesus.

8.  Ask God for the gifts of the Holy Spirit.

9.  Ask him for a revelation of his Word as you open and study it.

10. Intercede for others when you are in this place of his presence.

## Unconquered Code #6

Experience true power through daily surrender to Christ.

## Battle Action Step

Prayer is the lifeblood of communicating with God. In your prayer life today, begin to utilize the battle strategy in the code provided above.

## Discussion

1. Identify some areas of your life that you need to surrender to God.

2. How does surrendering your life to God empower you to live unconquered?

3. What would your life look like five years from now if you surrendered every pain, every battle, every challenge in your life, including your life, to God today?

## Prayer

*Heavenly Father, I am beyond grateful for another day, for another opportunity to serve you. More than anyone else in this world, you know my pain, and you know the scars and the hurt in my life. Today, I am coming to you in total surrender and asking you to take these things from me. I choose to surrender to you not because of my own intellect or because I'm being forced by others. It is my choice. I am yours. My life is yours. All my dreams, ambitions, all my past and tomorrows, they are all yours. Order my steps and lead me. Amen.*

*The best and most beautiful things in the world*
*cannot be seen nor even touched,*
*but just felt in the heart.*

HELEN KELLER[30]

## PRINCIPLE #7

# RELATIONAL POWER

*Therefore encourage one another and build one another up,
just as you are doing.*

1 Thessalonians 5:11 ESV

My friend Marcus Luttrell had just finished speaking and introduced me to everyone at the conclusion of his talk. The sound crew lit the fireworks from the stage and began to play a walkout video with the song "Back in Black" by AC/DC. As the announcer began to introduce me over the sound of music and fireworks, it felt more like I was walking into a wrestling match than speaking on stage.

Once I got up there, I. Was. Jacked. Up. I was ready to break bricks, run through walls, whatever, let's do this! There I stood in front of over one thousand law enforcement officers from all over the country in this enormous ballroom in a casino in the northeast US. Being nervous really isn't an issue for me when it comes to speaking, primarily because my sole concern is the people who are listening to me. My mission is to touch one person; there's usually at least one person who is present that needs something I am sharing that day.

When I began my presentation, I told a story about a mother lion and her cub, and I want to begin this chapter by sharing it with you here:

A mother lion and her cub strolled across the sub-Sahara African terrain as the midday sun bore down on their bodies. The heat seemed to hit from both directions, the sky and the dirt. It was so dry, so hot, and she was leading her cub to find some water nearby. While out on their walk, they encountered a group of rabid jackals. Now, no one jackal could take on this momma lion and her cub, but they are incredibly strategic in their approach. One small group appeared as a distraction while two other groups came off their right flank and from the rear. In a split second, things turned deadly. The momma lion was killed protecting her cub, and while the cub survived, he was alone. There were no other lions in the area; they had wandered too far from the pride.

That day and following, the cub stayed in one central location, seeking water, eating whatever insect or plant he could find, until a group of sheep wandered nearby. One of the lead sheep approached this young cub and offered him some food and cold water and invited him to travel with them. "We will protect you," the lead sheep said. "All you have to do is walk with us." So the cub walked with the sheep. Day after day, week after week, all this lion heard was how the sheep talked. He saw how they behaved in the face of danger, and he began to act just like them. "Bahhh, bahhh," not from the sheep but from this lion. Odd as it seems, he didn't know otherwise. Still, he had grown into a much larger animal.

One afternoon the sheep and their orphaned lion were attacked by another group of jackals. In the distance stood a much older lion, presumably the grandfather of this orphaned lion. He saw his grandson lion running in fear from jackals in the middle of a bunch of sheep, and it enraged him. Within a few minutes, the older lion reached the sheep and younger lion, and he grabbed this young one by the mane.

The older lion roared, "Do you know who you are?" But the young lion remained quiet, he was in shock, his heart stricken with fear. The older lion, still holding the youngster by the back of his mane, took him and put is face over a nearby body of water.

"*Look, look at this reflection. Do you not see? You are not one of them! You are different. You are not a sheep. You are a lion!*"

In the heart of the young lion something began to awaken. All this time, he had known deep down that he was different. He knew he never fit in with the flock of sheep, but he had no one else to rely on, so he ran with the ones who accepted him.

"Now, young one, let me hear you roar," the older lion said.

After a few attempts, the young lion let out a roar so majestic, so terrifying, it rattled the limbs on every tree nearby, and the dirt began to dance on the surface of the ground. He discovered who he really was and had regained his identity, and while he was grateful to the sheep, it was time to return to his pride.

Now, I'm not sure where this story originated because I have tried to find the source of it for years. It is one of the most powerful stories I have ever heard or shared.

After I finished sharing this story, I went on to share some of the pains from my life. I spoke with vulnerability, candidness, and passion. I am not a preacher, but the gospel is the core of who I am, so I shared with them that it was because of Jesus that I was standing in front of them. For nearly seven hours afterward, I talked with law enforcement officers, one-on-one, about topics of purpose, relationships, hope, love, and healing. There was so much more. Many reached out to me in the days that followed to share how our time together impacted their lives, and it has been, to date, one of the most memorable moments of my life.

I worked tirelessly on my presentation for that audience, one which I'd given numerous times in other locations, but I knew I had to bring my A game for this one. So I took that same talk to the next event, which I speak at every few months, in Ohio. For four hours I had the pleasure of talking one-on-one with first responders from all over the nation. So many people could relate to my points of pain, people who said my story gave them courage to face their own pain, and it motivated others to fight for their marriages and healing. One man came up to me after my talk and shared things with me he said he'd never shared with counselors, pastors, ministers, or anyone else.

Nowadays, I am humbled when I receive an email, text, or call from a first responder who has heard one of my talks. I am not saying this to brag in any way. I consider it an incredible honor to pour into the lives of these men and women, and the testimonies and their stories of victory bless me deeply.

What these messages and conversations remind me of is how much we need each other. It is an inhumane tragedy for people to go through their entire lives with nobody to share their pain, their joy, their victories, or their battles with. It is a tragedy for people to die alone. We must do better. We must remind our brothers and sisters they are not alone, and we are stronger, more resilient, and better together.

One of my favorite parts of closing out my talks at an event is when everyone, and I mean 100 percent of those attending, stand in support of every brother and sister in the room. They stand as a show of support, like a beacon of hope, saying, "You can call on me, and I will fight for you and with you!" It's always a moving moment! I love closing those moments out with something like, "And this is what makes you the greatest profession/men/women in the world!"

There are times when we will face battles in life we simply cannot endure alone. Proverbs 17:17 says it like this, "A friend loves at all times, and a brother is born for a time of adversity" (NIV). In law enforcement, you will hear many refer to each other—former, retired, and active—as brothers and sisters. That is not something said flippantly. It is earned. It is a way to recognize that if you are battling alone, I will be your backup. I will be there to stand with you, to walk beside you, to support you, to do whatever I can to help you through that adversity. If you are called "brother" or "sister," it is an honor. Do not take it lightly.

We need people in our lives who remind us of who we are, who will call out the best in us, who will challenge us when they see us living in sin, and, when we are prone to isolating ourselves from the world, who will sit with us as friends. We need people who will love us like Jesus, challenge us, empower us, influence us for good, and support us through it all.

## The Example of the Lion and the Lamb

As you read the story of the lion and sheep, maybe it brought to mind some people in your life who remind you of that older lion mentioned. When God sent his Son, Jesus, to this earth, he sent him fully God and fully man. This is an example of how he is compassionate. He chose to suffer with us, to suffer for us, so we could be reconciled back into a right relationship with the Father. Jesus spent more time walking with sinners than he did speaking from synagogues and beautiful platforms. While the religious teachers of that time were teaching laws and propositions in the temples, Jesus was walking with sinners. You see, Jesus acted relationally because he is relational, and every aspect of his assignment on earth was to restore relationships between humanity and God.

The standard for relational living has been set by the way Jesus walked with humanity during his time on earth and the way God continues to love us even in our sin. Everyone will have a different perspective of relationship with God, and for this, we look at Job. Job faced tremendous pain, and when tempted to curse God for it, he chose to worship him. Look at David, the adulterer and murderer. God declared him a man after God's own heart. He wasn't defined by his sin but by his repentant heart and pursuit of God.

We see how God is relational throughout the Bible, from Genesis to Revelation. The first instance is when God saw Adam alone and said it was not good for him to be alone, so he created Eve. Even today, in our modern society, many become emotional during weddings and funerals because we are relational at the center of who we are as human beings.

Jesus is both the Lion and the Lamb, and he relates to us in our brokenness and our bravery. For the men and women who serve, he sees your heart of courage, and for those who are not called to serve, he is gentle and kind for every need you have. Jesus is the relational standard.

In fact, it could be argued that he remained a few days after the resurrection to spend one last day with his friends on earth. This is who Jesus is: friend of sinners, accused of being many things by the religious crowd of his day, but all the while, he was and is our salvation!

In the twenty-first century, we can do more for the kingdom of God by walking out the gospel than we can within the four walls of a church. When Jesus said to follow him, he meant to follow his example. I believe he meant for us to follow his example of relational evangelism. It is impossible to share the gospel effectively without first having rapport with another. Without that common ground established, we lack the authority to speak into another person's life. Without love, we have no authority to speak into another person's life. It is because of love that we seek out and build relationships, to walk beside others so they are not alone in their journey. Walking beside another is more important than preaching at them.

## What's Love Got to Do with Anything?

When we hear the word *relationships*, we often, by default, think about romantic relationships. But we benefit from several different types of relationships throughout our lives, and each one is an example and demonstration of God's love for humanity. Throughout the Bible, we see where the Greeks used four primary words to describe four types of love we experience.

Our friendships, which is how romantic relationship begins, are defined as *philia* love in the Bible. This is the type of love Christians most often demonstrate toward each other. We see it mentioned here in 1 Thessalonians 4:9, "Now concerning brotherly love you have no need for anyone to write to you, for you yourselves have been taught by God to love one another" (ESV).

*Eros* love is the type of love displayed in romantic relationships. It is easy to see throughout the book of the Song of Solomon. But there are examples in Ecclesiastes also: "Enjoy life with the wife whom you love, all the days of your vain life that he has given you under the sun, because that is your portion in life and in your toil at which you toil under the sun" (Ecclesiastes 9:9 ESV).

The love we often see between parents and children, siblings, and throughout the family dynamic is *storge* love. When we lack *storge* love, it is *astorge*, which is found in Romans when defining the unrighteous. A lack of *storge* love is found in those who are heartless and, when it is lacking in families, is an additional sign of the end times.

And the fourth degree of relational power is that found in *agape* love. It is the Christlike, unconditional love. Now, each of these types of love should be found within a marriage, which is why marriage is so sacred and important and should be protected. It is about love and how we can experience the closest demonstration of God's love here on this earth.

Romantic relationships are relatively self-explanatory in that it is a dating relationship or marriage. While marriages should have both *philia* and *eros* love present, it is essential for the *philia* to be first because before you are lovers, you are best friends. Maintaining that friendship throughout the seasons of life is essential for a successful, thriving, healthy relationship.

It is impossible to follow Christ and not see how we were created for love, relationship, and togetherness. When Jesus was born, he was born into a family. God in the flesh was born into a family. Think about that. And for all accounts, in modern times, this would have been labeled a dysfunctional family. "What do you mean you didn't get her pregnant?" They would have fit right in with most!

While we can make it through life without romantic love, we need agape love, family love, and the love of each other. For without love, what is life? There is no hope without love. There is no eternity without love. It is love that drove Jesus to the cross for you and me. And it is love that causes us to hold each other up when we are facing challenges and what prompts us to call one another out when we are in sin.

## Relationships to Avoid

*Do not be deceived: "Bad company ruins good morals."*

1 CORINTHIANS 15:33 ESV

I want to preface this section by saying, first of all, we can't boot every single evil and corrupt person from our lives.

There are some situations where we have to hold our ground, know what we believe and stick by it, and stay in a spirit of prayer. If people in our lives gossip, they need someone who says, "I am not the person you need to share that information with. It is none of my business, and I would appreciate it if you would change the topic." If they are always negative, they need people who will be there and, in love, say, "Listen, there *is* hope. There is something good that can come out of this," and challenge their limiting beliefs. There must be a hard line you draw called boundaries. If people in your life do not respect those boundaries, then you must attempt to remedy it, and if not successful, then it may be time to see them less frequently.

One of my dear friends and a retired law enforcement officer, who happens to be my neighbor, says it like this, "If they don't make you better, they aren't your friends." If you are spending time with people who don't challenge you or people who are constantly draining you of energy, even relationships that are one-sided, it's time to evaluate those associations. If you are married and your relationship meets any of these, talk with your partner about it. See what you can do as an individual to contribute to a solution and begin working on it together. Avoid associating with people who constantly drain you of energy or who present any of these toxic signs:

1.  **Gossip:** If they gossip about someone to you, they will gossip about you to others.

2.  **Negativity:** They have a problem for every solution and cannot be positive.

3.  **Worry Feeding:** They do not encourage you, and they feed worry with more doubt and fear.

4.  **Lack of Support:** They never support any of your endeavors.

5. **One-Sidedness:** It's like the phone only works one way. Quit calling them first and see where you rank in their priorities.

6. **Energy Thieving:** There's never anything good, and you are always presented with a problem when you talk with them. You leave drained, exhausted, and needing to recharge.

7. **Manipulation or Control:** If they don't speak straight with you, if they are shady, or if you see where they are trying to control or manipulate you, it's time to create some distance.

I've heard many people say, "I date (him or her) because I want to witness to them and lead them to Jesus," even though they know the person is not good for them. We use the excuse that we want to be a positive influence in someone's life to continue hanging around them when we should be with our families or working on the goals we talk about. It is important to associate with like-minded people who will walk with you in life, and when you are around anyone who demonstrates any of the seven toxic signs, use caution. Toxic relationships could corrupt your morals!

## Embracing Healthy Relationships

Chances are, as you read the story about the lion and her cub, you recognized some similarities in your life. You think about the pain you've experienced and how you let it negatively affect you. Well, from one lion to another, you're not defined by your past. Period. And you don't have to be a prisoner to the pain. Unresolved wounds, unaddressed trauma, and attempts to suck it up for so long drive us farther from the pack and isolate us to the point of defeat. We need each other. There's not a single person in this world who is self-made. We need community, healthy relationships, and the humility to lean on one another when things are tough.

There's a lot of truth in this old fable of the cub and the sheep, and I love to share it when I speak to audiences anytime I get the opportunity. The fact is that sheep are incredibly dumb animals, and they must be led, whether on paths of righteousness or to the slaughter. We see this happening all throughout our society today, but no matter how society and culture change, there is only one Great Shepherd who truly cares for the flock.

Our social, professional, and spiritual life are based on relationships. During the holidays, we attend family gatherings even when there is someone present whom we don't like. We attend work functions outside of our normal duties. Many attend church, and it's all because of relationships, either to maintain the ones we have or to develop new relationships.

There are four key ways relationships serve us in this life, and I call them The Four Degrees of Relational Power:

- Relationships challenge us.
- Relationships empower us.
- Relationships influence us.
- Relationships support us.

## Relationships Challenge Us

> *As iron sharpens iron,*
> *so one person sharpens another.*
> PROVERBS 27:17 NIV

Entrepreneur and speaker Jim Rohn is often quoted as saying we are the average of the five people we spend the most time with. Whom we spend our time with is one of the greatest predictors of our futures. If you want to be successful in business, the people you spend the most time with should be successful in business. If you want a better marriage, you should surround yourself with people of your sex who are doing marriage the right way. You see where this is going. You are not created to be everyone else's mentor and coach, and if you don't have people in your life who will challenge you (Relational Degree #1), you will find it difficult to grow and advance in life. When we surround ourselves with people who challenge us and people who genuinely care about us, we are in a better position to achieve our goals and see our dreams become reality.

These four degrees of relational power won't always be four separate groups of people or four different relationships. You could have a small circle of friends, two or three people, and within this nucleus of your life, you see each of these relational degrees in action. And if you're blessed in your marriage, your spouse meets all these.

## Relationships Empower Us

*Above all, keep loving one another earnestly, since love covers a multitude of sins. Show hospitality to one another without grumbling. As each has received a gift, use it to serve one another, as good stewards of God's varied grace.*

1 PETER 4:8–10 ESV

In January of 2021, I received an email from someone known by many in the Louisville, Kentucky, area as the Prayer Lady. She asked me about my book *Behind the Badge: 365 Daily Devotions for Law Enforcement* and what it would take to get copies of the book into the hands of every officer at Louisville Metro Police Department. I won't mention her full name, but "Mrs. Prayer Lady" is one of the most incredible human beings you could ever meet. She worked in conjunction with a nonprofit organization in their area to secure one thousand copies to give one to each law enforcement officer who works for LMPD. I wish there were space here to begin sharing the testimonies resulting from her email and hard work. There are numerous testimonies. More than we can mention here.

One relationship turned into the opportunity to touch every officer in one department. You need people in your life who will empower you to achieve your goals and dreams, to walk out your purpose in life, and to allow God to use them. But on the other hand, maybe it is you whom God is wanting to use to help someone else see their dreams come true. If you have the opportunity and ability to help someone or open a door of opportunity for someone, do it.

## Relationships Influence Us

*Whoever walks with the wise becomes wise,*
*but the companion of fools will suffer harm.*

PROVERBS 13:20 ESV

You've heard it, and maybe you've said it: "I don't need anyone," or "I'd rather live alone than put up with people." It's a slippery slope to buy into such thoughts. As we become comfortable in isolation, we no longer have a heart of love for humanity much less for those closest to us. We are to use our gifts to serve one another. Friends who have good habits and good self-discipline lead by example, not by pushing certain behaviors down your throat; rather, their example influences you. You see other married couples and how they love one another, and it makes you want to be a better spouse.

## Relationships Support Us

*Though a man might prevail against one who is alone,*
*two will withstand him—*
*a threefold cord is not quickly broken.*

ECCLESIASTES 4:12 ESV

I have a small circle of close friends, but I have a large family of brothers and sisters across the nation. I've met thousands of them! I was recently speaking at an event in North Carolina when an entire team of men from a nonprofit organization came up to me and asked if they could pray for me. They asked me to sit in a chair, and they surrounded me and covered me in prayer. Some of the people I have been friends with since I was a kid have seen me at my absolute worst. They were there when I had nothing, when I talked about writing, and through every step of the way. We need friends who will walk with us through healing from traumatic experiences and pain as well. And to be that friend to someone else requires us to be compassionate and kind, considerate and caring. This is what separates friendships from acquaintances: compassion.

## Expanding Our Circle

While we need to have boundaries and recognize when it is time to no longer associate with some people due to their evil behavior, we should not let our past pain in relationships hinder us from experiencing the beauty found in godsent friendships and relationships. There is significant power in numbers, and when you are having a rough day or when you get a bad diagnosis from the doctor or on the day a loved one dies, you want someone who will walk with you, pray with you, and stand by your side.

Loyalty is rare. So is authenticity. If you want to develop real meaningful relationships, it requires vulnerability, authenticity, and loyalty. Expanding your circle of friends means stepping outside of your comfort zone and into arenas of like-minded people, where you can meet others who will challenge you and vice versa.

When it comes to relationships, they will either empower you or tear you down. It is your responsibility to protect your peace, protect your joy, and not allow others to rob you of those things. It is imperative that you set boundaries and stick to them. Cherish the healthy relationships you have, be grateful for them, but use discernment when associating with toxic people.

## Unconquered Code #7

Cherish your healthy relationships and distance yourself from toxic relationships.

## Battle Action Step

Identify the healthy relationships in your life. How can you maintain them?

## Discussion

1. Can you see signs of toxic relationships in your life?

2. What are some ways you can reciprocate friendship to those who have been there for you?

3. What kind of relationships do you believe honor God and help us further his kingdom?

## Prayer

*Heavenly Father, thank you for my family, my friends, and my loved ones. Thank you for surrounding me with people in my life who support me and help me grow closer to you. I ask you for the wisdom, discernment, and courage to identify those relationships that you want me to sever ties with so I can continue on the path you have laid out for me. Amen.*

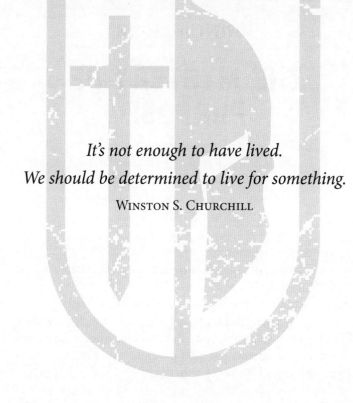

*It's not enough to have lived.*
*We should be determined to live for something.*

<small>WINSTON S. CHURCHILL</small>

# THE MYSTERY OF PURPOSE

*The LORD will fulfill his purpose for me;*
*your steadfast love, O LORD, endures forever.*
*Do not forsake the work of your hands.*

PSALM 138:8 ESV

To answer the question of purpose, I want to take you back in time about two decades, just before my world changed, and to a point in my life when pain was still the professor teaching me. I married my high school sweetheart, Amber, about five months after graduating high school in 2000. We were both eighteen years old, and I thought I had life by the horns. Her family loved and accepted me right away, and they have loved me so well for more than two decades, welcoming me as one of their own. But our high school love-story-turned-marriage didn't start out all roses and romance. During the first year of our marriage, I packed my bags to leave her once a week it seemed, at least any time an argument or conflict arose. A few months after our first anniversary, Amber and I divorced. We didn't have any children, and by all accounts, if you knew our situation, you would have thrown her a party and celebrated for her. I was toxic, and I didn't know it. I was wounded, unhealed, and unwell and cheated Amber of so much joy because of it.

After the judge finalized our divorce, I began to drink wherever I could find or get alcohol. I was pursuing relationships with anyone because I wasn't comfortable being by myself, and while I couldn't run from myself, the unhealthy relationships and alcohol served as a Band-Aid. I can tell you now how I was wounded and how incredibly toxic I was because I am well. I wasn't then but wasn't aware of it. My learned response to pain was to hide it and, if I couldn't hide it, to run from it. Because of this, our first year was unnecessarily brutal, and I accept full responsibility for it. The fact is that I was still a boy, a boy unhealed from pain, and all I knew was how to hide the wounds of my soul, the wounds you would never know existed if I never shared them with you.

One evening while at home and intoxicated, I opened the Bible Amber and I used to share during Sunday morning church service. Out of that Bible fell a little piece of paper, a love note Amber had written to me earlier in our relationship. It enraged me. I threw the Bible across the room as hard as I could and directed my rage and anger toward God, asking him if he thought it was funny. I asked him if that was his way of reminding me of my hurt.

One afternoon a few days later, I had gone for a long run at a local trail with a friend of mine who had walked with me through all the pain. We've not been as close in recent years due to busy schedules and running in opposite directions, but he mentored and guided me, kept me between the rails when I was running off the course of life. We were finishing our run and approaching our vehicles when Amber pulled up in her car. With tears running down her face, she chased me down and said, "Can we talk?"

I was hard-hearted. I was cold on the inside. And I was full of pride. "I ain't got a thing to say to you anymore," I replied and kept running. A few hours later, I called her. We met, went out for dinner that night, and attended a service at the church where our wedding was held.

That night I chose forgiveness. That doesn't make me a hero or some great person. It is a reflection of Amber, of her love, her compassion, and her kindness toward me. That's been more than twenty years ago, and I am thankful for the pain because it taught me how to forgive, how to love, and how to accept real love.

Now, I am sure that the more I have shared my story, the more likely it is that I have unknowingly become a case study for some mental health professionals. I say it jokingly, but it is likely, and that's fine. From day one, it seemed we were facing an uphill battle as a young married couple. Two kids, that's what we were, and all we thought we knew was love. What I didn't realize was I was married to someone who was a champion of love, and she taught me what that meant. Amber has walked with me through financial disaster and the loss of her brother, my grandfather, and many of our family members and friends over the past few decades. She's been with me through my healing from trauma and single-handedly allowed God to use her to refine my reckless and wild spirit into a force to be reckoned with.

She learned that love just like I learned it from her. She learned it from her family and from her own pain in life. She learned how not to treat folks. We never let a day go by without expressing our love for one another, and we try to cherish our time together as often as possible, knowing that to have the best and healthiest relationship, we must love well, forgive freely, and have fun together. We're not responsible for healing our spouses, but we are responsible for loving them well through the pain.

## A Lesson Unforgotten

One of the first of Amber's family members I met was her brother Wesley. He was a few years younger than Amber and a little older than their younger brother, Trent. He loved his friends and family, and I mean he loved them big time. He loved Auburn University football, and he loved his truck. Like any teenage boy, he wasn't perfect; he made his share of mistakes, like every one of us has made. But it didn't stop him from leaving one giant mark on the lives of many people.

One particular Friday night in the fall of 2004, after playing the trumpet in the marching band, Wesley became very sick, seemingly out of nowhere. His momma, Angie, had been a nurse for many years, and that night she noticed something just wasn't right about him. They discovered a large bruise on his side and rushed him to the emergency room. Doctors soon notified Wesley and his family that he was battling an advanced stage of an aggressive form of leukemia.

As the following weeks turned to months, Angie, Wesley, and his stepdad and family traveled to MD Anderson Cancer Center in Houston, Texas, where he was treated for leukemia. Along the way, he received donations from various organizations and individuals, but he didn't keep them for himself. Instead, he used the money to buy and give away some unique and special nickel-sized coins. In the center of each coin is an actual mustard seed, about the size of the tip of a fine point pen. On the back of the coin was the verse from Matthew 17:20, "He replied, '...Truly I tell you, if you have faith as small as a mustard seed, you can say to this mountain, "Move from here to there," and it will move. Nothing will be impossible for you'" (NIV). Wesley gave them to other patients in the hospital or at the Ronald McDonald House, where they lived during treatments, and to their family members, doctors, nurses, and anyone he met.

Wesley was an encourager, and to this day, so many people, including yours truly, continue to live with the profound impact he made on our lives. I am sure I am not the only one who continues to hold dear that tiny mustard-seed coin. Faith in God really does make all things possible. We are strengthened in our battles when we encourage others.

Shortly before Wesley received his heavenly reward, I recall someone asking him if there was anything he wanted, like a trip or a visit from a celebrity. There wasn't any type of stipulation. I don't recall every detail of the conversation, and I don't remember who all was present. Still, I vividly recall Wesley saying something that, to this day, is a compelling force in my life, and I hope it will be for you too.

When asked what he wanted, of all things, he didn't say a trip to some amusement park or to meet some celebrity. He said, "I want to grow up to be a husband and father."

I don't know if he knew his time was coming to an end or not. But, facing a battle with leukemia and with his body under so much stress from it and all the treatments, his priorities and purpose were clear. We take for granted the people who love us when someone in this world wants the chance to experience that type of love.

Maybe your dream isn't to be a parent or spouse, but you do have a plan and desires of your own. And at the core of who we are, we long for togetherness; we crave authentic love and genuine relationships. So one day, when we face the end of our lives, maybe we will have the chance to reflect on our lives and see that we loved well, were loved well, and didn't take for granted the most precious gift in this life: each other and love. In the end, we will all desire to linger a bit longer to be with the ones we love. Our purpose is to love those in our lives and love them well.

To this day, I still have an Auburn University hat I gave to him while he was fighting cancer. It is on my bookcase in my office in a clear protective box. Even though it's been more than fifteen years since Wesley passed, his response still impacts me. From time to time, I pay special attention to Wesley's hat when I sense I am losing my focus on what matters most in life. And, when things get hairy, I remember what he said about wanting to be a husband and father. I look in my home and see my wife and children, my family, friends, and loved ones and remember not to take for granted what matters most in life. His legacy continues to live on because his life and faith made me a better man. Thank you, Wes. I hope you know how much you have touched me, and I hope that I do justice to your dream.

## Build a Legacy That Serves

After Wesley's passing, his mother, Angie, advocated for the Leukemia & Lymphoma Society, raising money through various fundraisers and events. Her energy, passion, and commitment to honoring Wesley's life have inspired so many. To this day, her work and his life continue touching the lives of anyone who comes to hear of their story. My precious mother-in-law had to do the unthinkable by burying a child, and I watched as she grieved, as she grew, and as she healed. She loves her grandkids so well and strives to be present for all of them. There's a verse in Proverbs that is the most accurate description of Angie: "She is clothed in strength and dignity, and she laughs without fear of the future" (Proverbs 31:25 NLT). Today, she is still an incredible mother to Amber and Trent, and she is Nana to some amazing grandkids who adore her.

Wesley built a legacy but not one that would leave a school or a stadium named after him. His legacy cannot be measured with natural calculations. No, his legacy leads people to place their hope in Jesus, to discover a strong and deep faith once again, and to have courage in the face of adversity.

It's a legacy that serves both God and humanity. It's a legacy that will continue to touch lives around the world.

About eleven years after Wesley's death, I was invited to present for a local TEDx event in Alabama. They knew of my faith background and a bit about my story, so they were sure to tell me, "No religious talk." While I respected their organizational requirements, I knew I had a meaningful message, and I had to get it across quickly and effectively. Now, I was still very much new to speaking at the time, so my delivery and organization of content needed work. But, knowing I had less than twenty minutes to deliver a moving presentation, I decided to share the most important thing of all: the impact of love.

The title of my TEDx talk was "More Than a Masterpiece." I shared my personal stories of overcoming the pain of abuse and betrayal, but my focus was on sharing the story of Wesley. I told those in attendance that day what it meant to have a purpose, what it meant to love, and what we miss out on when we look for it in all the wrong places.

You may not see your life as a masterpiece. I get it. I was there at one point in my life too. Life is messy. It can also be chaotic, and it can be unspeakably painful. But it is and will always be precious. Are you viewing your life by measuring it against worldly success and achievement? If so, maybe that's why you can't see how magnificent yours is. Matthew 16:26 says it like this, "For what profit is it to a man if he gains the whole world, and loses his own soul? Or what will a man give in exchange for his soul?" (NKJV). What does it matter if you gain all the wealth, all the riches, climb to the peak of career success, but you lose who you are inside? Your relationships and life are worth more than success in business or finances, and your life is a masterpiece, covered with love, threaded with grace and mercy, forged in pain.

Look at your life through God's eyes. What do you see? You should first see his Son, Jesus, standing as your defense attorney before a judge, being prosecuted by the enemy of our souls, in a case for eternity. Next, you should see God declare you not guilty because of acceptance of the perfect sacrifice. You should see *you* restored to salvation, redeemed, empowered by perfect love.

Wesley lived a life that was a masterpiece.

And I am confident that the day he closed his eyes here on earth, he opened them in the presence of his Savior, and then he heard, "Well done! What a masterpiece!"

Live in such a way that you hear the same when your life is over. Live in such a way that you do not leave any regret, no unpursued dreams, and no unfulfilled calling or purpose.

## Magnificent Creator

One life changed the destiny of all humanity, of all who would say, "I believe." One life changed the future of the lives of men and women who would choose to follow him by faith. I believe we have been put here for a reason. When someone who is enduring pain asks me about their purpose, I like to put it to them like this: God the Father sent his Son, Jesus, to pave the way. He is the Way. He came so we could have eternal life, and he came to tear down walls, to break the chains off those enslaved to sin, and to empower those who would follow him.

When we were born, we were deployed from heaven to earth on a mission to continue the work of Jesus here on earth by sharing, through the way we live, the love he demonstrated. He came so we could live unconquered. He came so we would know our purpose, discover our calling, and live victoriously. Look at what the life of seventeen-year-old Wesley did for many people and imagine what you can accomplish through surrender!

## Perspective in Context

Throughout human existence, we have sought the answer to our reason for existing and how that relates to our purpose. Most often, when someone questions his or her purpose, it is, at least to some degree, tied to a perception of vocation. However, this is an incredibly shortsighted approach to such a profound and immeasurable issue. For example, if you opened a search engine browser today and typed "what is my purpose of existing," you would see there are more than two billion answers available.

Think about that for a moment.

Two. Billion. Opinions.

Some will tell you your purpose is associated with a career, while others will suggest it is to experience and express emotions. Many will say to you that your purpose is to marry and reproduce, while some say it is to explore the world. No wonder we wrestle with this issue so often. We're being fed so many views, opinions, and options that we don't know where to start. It's essential to keep it in perspective when seeking the answer, so we do not look at our purpose from the perspective of merely a vocational point of view. We must address it through the lens of eternity, and when we begin to see life through that lens, we will discover how close our purpose was to us all this time.

However, because we are busier than ever and our attention spans are often seconds long, it becomes more challenging to focus and quiet our minds. When our senses are constantly stimulated, the chaos prevents us from knowing what is closest to us. Because of the constant distractions in this world, we are robbed of the opportunity to discover our God-given purpose.

When our minds are constantly being stimulated, we have an even greater challenge to be still, be quiet, and hear the voice of the Great Shepherd. He still leads, but it is through the still, small voice. And where he leads, the enemy will attack. Where we have a need, the enemy will strike. John 10:10 says the enemy comes to kill, steal, and destroy. But he won't always show up while wearing a bandit mask with a weapon to kill us, a mallet to hit us over the head and steal from us. He won't necessarily show up with a wrecking ball to destroy our lives. No, he will show up subtly through the cracks of opportunity we give him, and he will begin his attack by distracting us. He will begin his attack by discouraging us. He will start his attack by dividing us.

Before he divides families, relationships, churches, or nations, he divides the minds of men and women. He splinters their hearts. He causes them to doubt their purpose and calling in life so that they are so intently focused on finding it that they miss it.

You discover purpose when your mind is united with the instructions of God's Word, renewed by reading it, and cleansed through the power of prayer.

When I was a lot younger, if a particular situation were associated with pain or discomfort, I would see that situation as outside of my purpose. I would think that was the "devil trying to get me," but it wasn't always the case. Sometimes it was because I was ignorant and stubborn. Your purpose isn't always found in a place of comfort, and most likely, it will be discovered at a point of great pain. Pain is a powerful teacher and one we can learn a lot from, lest we repeat it until we do.

We often measure our ability to make money, experience pleasure, or climb the ladder of success in a career field when seeking or attempting to define our purpose. But it's so much more potent than any of those options. However, God showed us in Genesis 1 that we *are* created to work to the degree we are physically able to work. And not all our work is paid work; maybe some of it involves volunteer work in your church or a community organization.

Your calling is most likely where you are. If we are married, we are called to be godly husbands and wives. If we are employed, we are called to be good employees. If we are parents, we are called to be good parents. Our calling and purpose will intersect when we are good stewards of what we have been given: opportunities, relationships, gifts, talents, or resources.

And our most significant breakthrough in life is when we discover that it is not our purpose we seek; rather, we seek the pathway to surrender so we can live out his purpose for our lives.

## A Masterpiece of Life on Purpose

You are more than a bundle of a million emotions. You are the only known creation who can go beyond the ability of simply existing. You can think, choose, decide, and love, which is one of the greatest miracles of all.

Think for a moment about the last time you physically stood in a desert or on a beach. You felt the sand beneath your feet, and as you would take a step or move your feet, you could feel the grains of sand shifting with your movement. Grabbing a shovel or even a piece of heavy machinery, you could begin digging as hard and fast as possible until you reached layers well beneath the surface of the earth.

In contrast, when was the last time you looked into the sky at night, on a clear night, when you could see the stars? The longer you stare at the sky, the more stars become visible to your eyes. Now, take a telescope; they become more apparent. It now becomes possible to see things you never knew existed.

There are infinitely more stars in the sky than grains of sand on the earth. According to a 2003 NPR article, there are approximately "70 thousand million, million, million stars in the observable universe."[31] That article also mentions that, in his book *Spectrums*, author David Blatner shares how this equates to multiple stars for every grain of sand on planet earth, and while that seems impossible to fathom, there are more molecules than that in just a few drops of water. I cannot fathom 70 thousand million, million, million as a number, much less that many stars, all of which vary in size.

Now some may think that if we are so small, hanging in the balance of the vastness of all the heavens, then we aren't that significant. On the contrary, I see it like this: God saw one tiny molecule of water, not even visible to the naked human eye, and said, "I will send my best to redeem that." Just like that, he saw us, you and me, out of everything that has ever been or ever will be, and he chose us to love, to redeem, and for a purpose.

Yet we wonder why we exist.

Yet we wrestle with the question of our significance.

Out of all he created, he gave *us* his breath. He gave *us* his best; he gave *us* his love. God has not only instilled in us the need to work, but he also demonstrated rest. Our quest for living a life of purpose and fulfillment will require the balance of work and rest. It's a rhythm we must discover.

What incredible disappointment to believe, amid such endless creation, that we are here for such a short time to fulfill something only limited to this life or a vocation or even worse—making money.

## Love and Purpose

More magnificent than life is love. It is the power behind the words spoken in Genesis 1 that sparked this entire creation. First, we must experience the love of God outside the realm of an emotional response. We must have an experience based on total surrender of every fiber of our being to the Creator of it all, *Elohim*. Total, absolute surrender. When we experience his love, we discover real life!

Remember when I shared my patrol car experience? From that moment on, my purpose was to help others experience that same love however I could, specifically through speaking and writing.

And that's it; we have to experience his love before we can love ourselves, and we have to learn to love ourselves before we can love others. It's not a self-centered love; rather, it is a realization that the one who gave us breath loved us so much that he sent his very best, his own Son, so we could be restored to a relationship with him.

Authentic, divine love is the baseline for our existence.

Without that love and without having experienced love, our lives are empty. So, from the lens of a limited human perspective, and no matter how intellectual we may be, we can sum up our existence with one word: *love.* Such a powerful force spelled in four letters from one language among thousands on one planet among countless others. For thousands of years, brilliant minds have attempted to answer this question of the purpose or the reason for living. So if you are struggling with it, you're in good company. Be a good steward of your gifts, talents, time, and life. Multiply them. Grow them. Use them for good. Use them to honor God.

## Your "Why"

If I asked you why you chose your current career path or why you serve, you would likely answer with something closely associated with "I wanted to help others." But is it more profound than that? Our "why" is the reason we get up every single day. It's what drives you; it's a passion no other can understand. It will prompt you to make sacrifices to accomplish something, no matter how difficult, how challenging, or how long it takes.

- Why does the gunsmith make guns?
- Why do we put shoes on our feet every day?
- Why do we eat?

Looking at these three questions, we understand three things: One, there are practical answers to some of the most challenging questions in life. Two, we do things often without wondering why. And three, there's a reason for everything. Now, if we were sitting across from one another and I asked you why you do whatever work it is you do, you would likely tell me you do it so that you can put food on the table. We eat when we are hungry so we can nourish our bodies. We put shoes on our feet so we can walk without injuring ourselves. We do work because it is meaningful or at least in hopes that it will lead us to the place of meaningful work.

We are seeking to understand why we do what we do. Even when we don't understand, we are seeking it. Our souls crave to engage with divine purpose, and when we fail to do so, we become miserable in every way.

No one else can define your "why," and without it, you will never have a clear understanding of your purpose on earth, and you will always lack a vision for life. In his book *Find Your Why: A Practical Guide for Discovering Purpose for You and Your Team,* author Simon Sinek says, "The WHY can help set a vision to inspire people. The WHY can guide us to act with purpose, on purpose."[32] That's the importance of us answering this question: Why?

We can't allow ourselves to settle for the easy way out and say, "I don't know." That's lazy. Find out why you do what you do in life and be honest. If it's money, then acknowledge it. If it's for fame, then say it. If it's for power, lay it out there. Find your why, and you will discover a roadmap to purpose. Discovering what motivates us will reveal if there are areas of our life we need to adjust. For example, if you are motivated solely by making money, your purpose will remain undis-covered. Our motivation will be the answer to why we do certain things in life, and it will often lead us to a path of understanding our purpose.

Your life is precious. I know many people reading this have experienced trauma and may not see life the same way. But even those circumstances will serve you if you allow them. If you will allow those challenging places in life to make you better in some way, you can use them for good. Our purpose is not found in a career, although that career can be a vehicle for a season that enables us to operate in our divine purpose. Think from an eternal perspective and think about what really matters. I believe you will see that what really matters is faith, love, hope, and each other. Leave no regret; show your love; live on purpose.

## Unconquered Code #8

Seek to know your divine and unique purpose in life and the direction God is leading you to take.

## Battle Action Step

If today you were facing the end of life, what is one thing you would ask for?

## Discussion

1. List your passions in life (what you love doing or experiencing).

2. Write down your natural gifts and talents. (Is it art, speaking, writing, a trade, or another skill?)

3. What are some ways you can begin to live in alignment with God's plan for your life in conjunction with your passions, gifts, and values?

## Prayer

*Heavenly Father, I have so many questions about life. Today, I choose to open my heart, my mind, and my hands and ask you to lead me. Reveal to me the divine purpose for which you created me. Order my steps and lead me. Let me live in such a way that honors you and leaves no regret when my time here is up. Amen.*

*We must all suffer from one of two pains:*
*the pain of discipline or the pain of regret.*
*The difference is discipline weighs ounces*
*while regret weighs tons.*

JIM ROHN

## PRINCIPLE #9

# THE ANTIDOTE FOR COMPLACENCY

*The more self-discipline you have, the more you do the things you should do, the happier your future self will be.*

MAXIME LAGACÉ[33]

To serve in any capacity as a first responder or in the United States Armed Forces, candidates are required to pass an initial assessment and training phase. In law enforcement, candidates must pass a battery of tests, including a physical agility test. However, this test is merely a gauge of whether your body can last the first thirty minutes of the first day of the police academy. It is not indicative that your physical fitness and conditioning levels are superior. It is the minimum requirement. My first day at the police academy was chaotic, intentionally and purposefully designed to test the mental and physical abilities of those who wanted to become law enforcement officers. I quickly learned my preparation did not give me an edge; rather, it enabled me to survive.

Candidates are met on day one with abundant physical training, yelling, running, and chaos. But as the days and weeks progress, it seems things are beginning to get easier when, in fact, they are not. Your mind and body are becoming stronger and more familiar with the daily routine the instructors have prepared for you. It is meant to be challenging, intended to make you stronger and teach you how to survive on the streets. In addition, the instructors are there to instill a new level of discipline in each candidate.

The first few years of my career in law enforcement after the police academy, I would fold and put away my laundry because I was accustomed to it being done a certain way from training. I polished my boots every few days, made sure all my gear looked new, and kept my uniforms in pristine condition. I set a personal expectation for myself to train at least five days a week by running the trail or training in the gym. Going to the gym to get "in shape" is one thing; training for the fight of your life is another. I would always use a mind movie scenario to motivate me in the back of my mind. I would think something like, "This could be the day," referring to the possibility that I may have to fight for my life or someone else's life.

Disciplined cops are good cops, and disciplined people, in general, are more productive and healthier people. But too often, busy shifts, busy families, stress, and a myriad of other issues in life will keep us from maintaining that level of self-discipline we had at the beginning of our careers. While work and rest are essential, we must guard against laziness and complacency with the defense of discipline.

If you have discovered your motivating factors and reawakened that desire within to win in life again, this will be something that excites you! The day I graduated from the academy, I was squared away; I was in great physical condition, was disciplined, had a routine, knew what I needed to do to win every day, and was willing to do it. Awaken the warrior within you, find the will to fight again and the desire to live again. Rekindle the zeal and fervor for life and find your passion to win! Discipline comes easier when it is associated with a goal you are passionate about achieving. The single greatest weapon you have against complacency is self-discipline.

Death occurs the day we surrender to complacency. We may not cease to exist on that day, but it is just a matter of time. Complacent people are dead people waiting to die. Lazy people are defeated people waiting to lose.

Not everyone has the privilege of serving in the military or being a first responder. So maybe the story of going through the law enforcement academy didn't resonate with you, and if that's the case, let's look at it from a few different angles. If you're married, look at the day you were engaged. You didn't want to get married because of health benefits and a retirement package (at least I hope not!). You wanted to get married because you were both deeply in love with each other. You could probably talk until the early morning hours, and it seemed there was never a moment when you didn't have anything to say to each other. As the years passed, maybe that passion faded. Maybe you let life, stress, bills, kids, or other things in life get in the way of protecting that relationship. Complacency sets in. You may not divorce, but your marriage won't be the best it could be.

Do you remember the first time you went to church and decided to change your heart and your behavior? You chose to have faith and change your behavior because you wanted to go a different way in life. You were full of zeal and committed to reading your Bible daily and praying often. Then you grew cold. The zeal faded. Complacency set in.

The reality is that nobody achieves anything worth having in life without discipline. You will not achieve your personal health goals, your relationship goals, or your career goals, and you won't grow in faith without discipline. Nobody else can do it for you. It must be a decision and commitment you make, and it must involve an understanding of *why* you are making it in the first place. Remembering that *why*, like I talked about in the previous chapter, will keep your feet moving when your motivation is waning. That's what discipline is: doing what you know you need to do to achieve some goal, even when you don't feel like it.

## How Habits Affect Our Lives

Good intentions produce no good fruit. Only decisive action and consistent, effective behavior will lead to victory. Too often we think of habits in our lives as rigid behavioral requirements, things we dread doing, but this is not always the case. Habits are best defined as the actions you take daily without being aware of those actions. Our experiences and responses to various situations have developed specific, programmed responses to most stimuli. Through addressing motivating factors, addressing desired goals and outcomes, and tying those things to adjusted behaviors, we can effectively change our lives through proper healthy habits.

To live unconquered will require you to make some necessary adjustments. For one, think about how you begin and end each day. Do you wake up and hit the snooze button before jumping out of bed and rushing off to start your day? Lt. Col. Dave Grossman calls this your first battle of the day. Do you choose to let a button beat you, or will you start the day with a win? Refuse to give in to the allure of comfort and continued rest. Pursue your day with passion. The way you start your day will set the tone for your day.

You can have all the good intentions in the world, but intentions don't change behavior. Decisive action is the only thing that changes behavior, and it must be associated with an identifiable goal and purpose. Start your day with a goal and purpose!

ScienceDaily[34] published an article from *Society for Personality and Social Psychology* on the topic of habits entitled "How We Form Habits, Change Existing Ones." In their study on habits, the authors mention how public service announcements, educational programs, workshops, and weight-loss programs are all designed to improve our daily habits. However, the survey regarding an educational program designed to encourage eating more vegetables showed only 35 percent of people who were polled said the program affected their beliefs. They intended to change, but only 11 percent actually made a decision to eat five servings of vegetables a day. Programs and education may affect our intentions, but they will not change behavior.

One of the things that has helped me to change bad habits is replacing those habits with something better. Several years ago, I began drinking alcohol every night. Once I made a change in my life, I knew I needed to stop using alcohol to cover up my pain. Instead of drinking, I began writing. Another bad habit was drinking a lot of soda during the day when I was traveling or on the road. I knew I needed to switch to water, but it was incredibly difficult to chug a gallon or two of water a day. So I began putting bottles of water in various places where I could find them and easily grab them. I also began drinking sugar-free sodas during certain times of the day instead of using them for some type of comfort when I was stressed.

The greatest change came a few years ago when my doctor ordered some lab work, and the results were not good. My cholesterol levels were high, and my red blood count was high. He said I was a ticking time bomb waiting to have a stroke, heart attack, or some other major health issue. No, I am not fat-shaming anyone, but I was fat. I had become sloppy and unkempt. My mind wasn't as sharp either. My dad, who is one of my absolute best friends, had a heart attack and triple bypass heart surgery in his late forties. I wanted to learn from what Dad went through and set a better example for my kids. I knew losing weight through healthier habits would make him proud.

## The Antidote for Complacency

I had started this journey several times, but after a speaking engagement in Minnesota in January 2021, I saw a picture of myself on stage, and between that and the blood work the doctor ordered, it was time to make a change. From February 2021 to December 1, 2021, I lost fifty-three pounds of body fat, gained thirty pounds of muscle, and corrected every negative issue on my lab work. Thanks to a team of trained experts in my gym, specialists in Pensacola, Florida, and the support of my family and friends, I feel better than ever, and I am getting stronger every day.

It started with going to the gym at the same time every day. Throughout my entire adult life, I have often exercised in some manner or another, but in January 2021, I began training with a new purpose and mindset. I knew I would not have the energy to start and would need some help, so I restarted a pre-workout routine that I've had since January 2018. I also knew once I finished my workout, I needed some bait to look forward to. So I began using the same post-workout drink and protein. After a few months, I changed it up a bit for variety but kept the same routine. I didn't hold myself to a super-strict diet although I did cut out 98 percent of all sodas, processed foods, and sweets. I allowed myself to cheat once I achieved a goal. I used to have a "cheat day" once a week but found it to be more difficult to get back on track. The problem with becoming too slack and having frequent nutrition cheat days is that it can lead to complacency. Complacency is the single greatest predictor of someone who will experience defeat, and that is second only to those who quit.

Learn from my experience here: if you have a bad habit of hitting the snooze button in the morning, set six alarms, each one minute apart. Put the alarm across the room. The night before, cut out caffeine about three hours before bed at a minimum and eliminate screen time about an hour before bed. Do your best to make the room where you sleep as dark as possible and use an eye mask if necessary.

Finding the opportunity to change habits in your life requires more than intention; it requires decisive action and effort. Do it for more than one day or one week. Forget about whether it takes three weeks or three years to build a habit. Focus on the goal. Focus on the prize. Focus on what benefits will come from the new changes in your life.

As I looked over the experiences of my life, I discovered patterns, and I discovered the point where things began to change for the better. The biggest impact in my life came when I surrendered my life to God and things changed from the inside of me (will, thoughts, emotions). But even God won't force you to change the bad habits in your life. Discipline led to me creating some healthy routines, things that affected every area of my life. Here are the four areas in which determined discipline has been most critical in my life.

## 1. Spiritual Habits

Spiritual endeavors help us to understand the world and our place in it and form a comprehensive view of existence. Both philosophy and theology try to explain the fundamental nature of reality, and they can help us create a spiritual (i.e., big picture) understanding of the world.

The focus of spirituality is beliefs. Some examples of this would be religious observances, reading Scripture, personal beliefs (about the existence of God, the meaning of life, life after death, the law of attraction, etc.), ethical values, world peace, humanism, volunteer work, or life philosophy. Everyone believes something, and that belief system is what defines your values. But those beliefs can change through crisis, or you can become more deeply rooted in them. Your convictions must guide you. When beliefs become convictions, then habits become natural. Nobody fights for beliefs, only for convictions. I operate on a relationship with Jesus because he saved me when most had given up on me. No one else could reach me in my deep pit of pain. I always thought that being spiritual or a follower of Jesus made me weak and passive as a warrior, but it doesn't. I discovered faith makes me unbeatable. From this discovery grew my conviction that we can all live unconquered.

Our belief system and our deep convictions will either limit us in life or lead us to freedom, fulfillment, and victory. Your belief system may be different from mine, even if we are both followers of Jesus. We may see other issues differently within the Christian faith. And maybe you're not a follower of Jesus. Your belief system is what guides you and is the point of your values. I've shared how I came to a relationship with Jesus, and it wasn't like what anyone would expect.

As human beings, we don't want to simply know the *what*; we want to know why, who, and every detail of existence. Knowing our strength comes from faith in God grants us the power to delve into these questions.

Here are a few habits you can implement to help you along the way in this area of your life:

- **Daily Meditation:** One minute or one hour, it doesn't matter. Find time to quiet your mind. Consider a specific Scripture passage to dwell on or the victories you've experienced. Visualize the goals you have and the dreams coming to reality. Begin to think like you are already there, and then celebrate as though it has already occurred.

- **Prayer:** This may integrate with the daily quiet time that will help to soothe your soul and mind. When you pray, do not let it be a ceremonial approach. Because of Jesus, we can approach this boldly. God understands your language, and he hears your heart. Do not allow the formalities with which you may have been accustomed to rob you of this powerful communication line with God.

- **Daily Scripture Reading:** I highly recommend using a Bible app. It is one of the easiest tools to implement in your daily life. Find one that lets you set a reminder for yourself, and the app will send you a notification. Take a few minutes a day to get quiet, read Scripture, meditate on it, and pray.

## How to Pray

A common question I have received from people over the last few years relates to prayer. So many have asked me, "How do I pray?" While I am not an expert on prayer, I do have a method I have used for a while. For me, the key isn't to make any of this about performance or another box to check off so we can feel accomplished. Rather, it's about aligning our hearts and minds with that of God and his Word so we can live each day on the path he leads us down.

I always direct people to follow the example of Jesus. He revealed a pattern of prayer in the New Testament. Look at this from the Gospel of Matthew 6:9–13 (NIV):

> This, then, is how you should pray:
> "Our Father in heaven,
> hallowed be your name,
> your kingdom come,
> your will be done,
>     on earth as it is in heaven.
> Give us today our daily bread.
> And forgive us our debts,
>     as we also have forgiven our debtors.
> And lead us not into temptation,
>     but deliver us from the evil one."

Take the first line of Jesus' prayer, "Our Father in heaven," as the first step in this pattern. We must recognize him as Father, but often, pain keeps us from seeing him as such. He is good, regardless of the trouble we have in this world or the pain we experience in our lives. He doesn't need us to tell him he is holy, but our prayers demonstrate reverence, and reverence is due. No matter what you've experienced in life, he is good, he is perfect love, and he cares for you. He has not caused any of your pain, but he has been with you through it all. See him as a good, holy, and loving Father who will fight for you.

Second, "your will be done on earth as it is in heaven" acknowledges God's sovereignty and will over our desires. This is a difficult position to take from a natural mind, but if we intentionally serve him with open hands to heaven, he will do more with what little we have to offer than the best we could ever muster! His will may not align with yours, and that is okay.

"Give us today our daily bread" is a request to meet *today's* needs. He is our provision always, but we are taught to trust him daily. After all, that's how we live this life—not one year at a time, not ten years, but one day at a time. Trust him for today and don't worry about tomorrow. When we learn to trust him with today, we can trust him with tomorrow and all our past.

As we spend time in prayer, it is good to take a step of faith, in obedience, to forgive those who have harmed us, as we request forgiveness from God for our sins.

Then Jesus prayed, "Lead us not into temptations, but deliver us from the evil one." How often do we begin our days asking him to lead *us* not into temptation and to deliver us from the Evil One? Again, we do this by acknowledging him as our heavenly Father, his sovereignty, and his lordship over our lives. This does not mean we will not experience temptation, but we will be prepared for those tests. And while the Evil One rules this world, we will have the mind to resist him when that battle presents itself.

## How to Study the Bible

There are varying schools of thought on how we should read the Bible. Some suggest reading from several books and chapters a day, while others suggest reading in chronological order. My approach is with childlike faith, to explore, take the adventure, and experience his Word come alive in me. The Bible is a collection of books, sixty-six to be exact. Resist any temptation to approach this study with mere intellect. Approach this study in faith, knowing you cannot yet see what will come from it or understand it, but you will.

The best way to approach this is by setting aside some time each day. We cannot expect a preacher to give us all we need from God's Word during a thirty- or forty-five-minute sermon once a week. We must develop an appetite for studying God's Word. Daily Bible reading plans are a great way to develop a Bible reading habit. For you to get started, here is a daily *Unconquered* reading plan: Begin by reading one chapter of Proverbs a day and one to three psalms per day. Do this for the first thirty-one days. Once you finish the first thirty-one days, begin reading the book of Matthew in the New Testament while reading one chapter from the Old Testament and preferably a chapter from Psalms.

It is important to study Scripture in context, meaning don't look at only one verse and run with it without looking at the entire chapter and background behind the verse. There is significant depth to studying the Bible, and there are layers of wisdom and mystery to be discovered. When reading Scripture, ask the Holy Spirit to reveal the truth of God's Word to you, to show you the power of his Word. It's more than a historical book; it's alive and the most powerful book you will ever study.

Be sure to note that the Old Testament was originally written in the Hebrew language, while the Greek language was the original writing for the New Testament. You can search for a reliable lexicon that will help you discover the original meaning of the words used in the ancient language in which it was written. This will provide you with a deeper understanding of Scripture. Another helpful resource is a reliable commentary, through which you can obtain further insight from various scholars and theologians throughout Scripture.

## 2. Relationship Habits

To those who are married: be intentional about communicating with each other. Never leave "I love you" unsaid and always greet and depart with an embrace. Practice thoughts of kindness, love, and gratitude toward each other, which lead to actions of kindness and love. Never allow the stress of life to rob you of intimacy. Fight for each other, fight to protect the sacredness of your marriage. Your legacy is not born in your work; it is born in your home.

Communicate with your friends and family. Everyone is busy, and that is robbing us of authentic relationships and quality time together. Be diligent about being present with each other while you have the time together. Forgive freely and quickly. Cut ties with toxic relationships and cherish those who care for you and who make attempts to show up for you in life.

- **Communicate Often:** Talk to each other regularly. It requires effort in a world that is constantly vying for our attention and energy.
- **Be Present in the Moment:** Put the phone down. Look at each other. Create some boundaries for technology and eliminate the presence of them while sharing a meal together or in the bedroom.
- **Daily Huddles:** Come together as a family once a day, around a meal, by video, whatever you have to do. Continuing family legacies will require work in this age. It requires effort. There are too

many things pulling us in different directions, and we must learn to set boundaries and say no to other things and people so we can give our best yes to those we love.

- **Find a Mentor:** Seek someone who has accomplished what you desire. People in successful marriages mentor married couples. Successful business owners mentor new business owners. Find those of similar faith and belief systems and build a relationship where you can learn from their experiences.

### 3. Physical Habits

You will make time to care for your body, or your body will become your tyrant. Don't begin by sprinting here or setting lofty and unrealistic goals. Start with baby steps and build on a healthy foundation. This is not the most important habit, but it is important. If you haven't seen a doctor for a physical and lab work in a long time, make that a priority soon. I would like to take time to thank Lt. Col. Dave Grossman for his advice and suggestions relating to sleep and habits for better sleep:

- Be active twenty to thirty minutes a day, walking, running, training in a gym.
- Drink water when you first awaken.
- Track your sleep; track your daily steps.
- Reduce caffeine intake at least three hours before bed.
- Eliminate screen time one hour before bed.
- Practice the box-breathing technique mentioned in Principle #3 a few minutes per day.

## 4. Mindset Habits

Are your thoughts stuck on repeat? When was the last time you challenged a thought instead of allowing it to ruin your day?

- Set a few reminders on your smartphone to say, "Is your thinking helping you grow or keeping you from growing?"
- Stop negative self-talk; no more "I can't do this," "I am stupid," etc.
- Start today by reaffirming that you have worth, that you have value, and that you are loved.
- Speak life into your situations; there is power of life and death in the tongue.
- Here are a few affirmations to help you in developing positive mindset habits:

  - I *am* lovable.
  - I *am* good enough.
  - I *am* loved.
  - I *am* beautiful/handsome.
  - I *am* strong.
  - I *am* an overcomer.
  - I see life as beautiful and meaningful.
  - I *am* unconquered.

These affirmations are merely words if you do not practice them in thought and deed. They are in line with the verse that "you are more than a conqueror" (see Romans 8:37). Your decisions will reflect your thoughts and view of yourself and your life. Once they are aligned with what God says about you, then they become empowering words and thoughts. You cannot live unconquered until you address a negative mindset and thought pattern.

## Self-Discipline Takes Hard Work

The most effective antidote to complacency in life is self-discipline. You are living in a world where people now think that just because they exist, someone owes them an opportunity or something else. Entitlement leads to laziness. Laziness leads to complacency. Disciplined individuals are not lazy; rather, they fight for what they stand for in life. No, this isn't easy. But it *is* possible. Commit to working on one of these four areas of your life. Don't try to tackle all these areas at once as you may become frustrated and quit.

On the note of frustration, it is the gateway to defeat. When you are frustrated, don't quit and don't make knee-jerk decisions based on your current state. Pause, take a step back, and clear your mind. Why are you frustrated? The most likely reasons are that the things you've been doing haven't worked or that you are not seeing the progress you envisioned.

There have been a lot of people in the Christian faith who have perverted the power of our speech, thoughts, mindset, and faith. They have used it for monetary gain and personal benefits. However, at the root of their misguided actions is a true source of incredible power. The reality here is that I am no different from you. If I can stop allowing alcohol and past pain to control my life, you can too. If I can write seven books in three years, you can too. Your success at this is determined by your willingness to shake off old and unproductive thoughts, ways, and habits and unlearn what has not worked.

Many successful individuals have used these habits in their lives to launch careers, improve relationships, start businesses, write books, and much more. Many inventions have come from the minds of those perceived as average people. My journey down this path of living unconquered was born out of my desire to rise above an average mind and intellect and become, to the fullest, the person God created me to be.

In today's world, some would suggest that you can do what you want without consequence. They would say that you can be whoever you want to be, do whatever you want to do, and that nothing is off-limits. So many are ultrasensitive and cowardly. Cowards don't inherit the kingdom of God. Cowards refuse to discipline themselves and submit to the lordship of Jesus. Cowards talk a good game but never show up on the battlefield. They criticize those in the arena while shaking in their boots at the thought of having to enter it themselves.

Choose to discipline yourself, or someone else will be given that authority over you. Today is your day of salvation. Today is the day you can start the process of winning again in life. Today is the day you shake off the old, defeated mind-set and embrace the way of the unconquered.

What will you choose?

## Unconquered Code #9

Accept responsibility for creating healthy daily habits of discipline in your life.

## Battle Action Step

Focus on one of the four areas mentioned in this chapter to begin implementing habits to live unconquered. Implement two to three of those habits from that focus area in your life.

## Discussion

1. Can you commit to improving at least 1 percent each day in one of the focus areas of life mentioned in this chapter?

2. How does a disciplined person honor God and lead a life of victory?

3. What steps can you take today to begin implementing a victory strategy in one of the focus areas of your life?

## Prayer

*Heavenly Father, thank you for new opportunities to grow in my faith in you. I am coming to you today and asking you to make straight those paths I have made crooked. Help me to correct the areas of my life where I have lacked discipline and send me a godly mentor who will lead me to a closer relationship with you. Amen.*

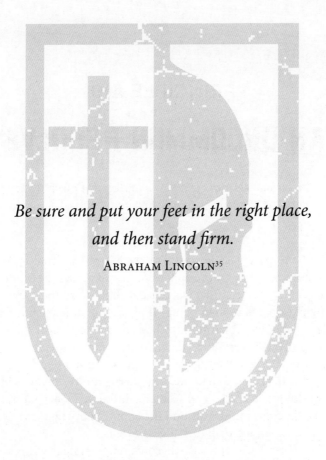

*Be sure and put your feet in the right place,*
*and then stand firm.*

ABRAHAM LINCOLN[35]

## PRINCIPLE #10

# AN UNCOMMON RESOLVE

*Victorious warriors win first and then go to war, while
defeated warriors go to war first and then seek to win.*

Sun Tzu[36]

Over the past decade, I've had the pleasure of talking to
thousands of law enforcement officers all across the United
States. I hear stories that would send chills down the spine of
any reasonable human being. If you're unfamiliar with the
day-to-day lives of American law enforcement, you should
know that it is very unpredictable. At some moments, it can
be as boring as watching water evaporate, and other days are
filled with absolute chaos. At a moment's notice, anyone's life
can change, and men and women who serve in law enforcement in communities around the country have an increased
risk of experiencing life-changing events.

There's one story I've become more familiar with over
the past few years. A southern Georgia deputy sheriff, who
had survived a line-of-duty injury after someone shot him,
connected me with Houston Gass. Houston has an incredible testimony, and his story will move you. When I think of
someone with uncommon resolve, I'll tell you, he comes to

my mind. Are there others? You'd better believe it, but what happened on January 6, 2015, was a defining moment for him.

In an interview with Houston Gass, he shared how on that day, January 6, a shift at his department was short-handed, and he was called in to work early. Anytime you have lieutenants and sergeants responding to calls, it's because they are short-staffed, which has become an even more serious issue since 2020. Around 10:45 in the morning, once he reported for duty, he was told of a domestic disturbance with shots fired, involving one male suspect and one female victim. He called his wife and told her their lunch date wouldn't happen because of the domestic disturbance, and more units were called in to assist.

Once Houston and his team arrived on the scene of the disturbance, they made several attempts at contacting the male suspect. While they didn't make contact, they were able to get the woman out of the home safely. Once they made entry, they searched throughout the house until Houston, three other officers, and a lieutenant behind them guarding against an ambush got to the southwest bedroom of the residence, toward the back of the structure. There was a bed against the wall and a door and couch close by. It was a cramped room, Houston shared.

As they made their way to the next room next, Houston began to open the door. As soon as he laid his hand on the doorknob, he was shot through the door with a 12-gauge shotgun point-blank in his face. Of this moment, Houston said, "It changed my life and the life of my family. My wife, Jessica, and our three children had their world turned upside down. While that day could be said to be my worst, I choose to look at it as my best. I am an unapologetic Christian, husband, father, survivor, and police officer!"[37]

Growing up, Houston's oldest sister was murdered, and his other sister died by suicide. His father died of cancer, and just like a lot of other couples, Houston has been through a previous divorce. Still, Houston stands firm on his faith, saying that after January 6, 2015, he became more deeply rooted in a relationship with Jesus, and he raves about the support and strength of his wife. I asked Houston what was one thing that sticks with him to this day since his shooting. He shared Exodus 14:14 with me: "The LORD will fight for you; you need only to be quiet" (paraphrase). If you met Houston, you'd see the scars that remain after nearly two dozen surgeries over several years. You'd also see a radiant smile and a man who, behind the badge, loves his wife, loves his God, and loves serving as a law enforcement officer. His story is a reminder that you don't have to allow your circumstance to define you, and you have a choice of how you handle what you face.

There's a lot we can learn from the story of this native Texan and a lot we can apply in our lives. With the smell of gunpowder still lingering, he made a decision in the moment of truth; instead of surrendering to the pain and injuries, he chose to fight a different way. He chose to place his hope and faith in Christ alone.

The American Psychological Association defines *resilience* as "the process of adapting well in the face of adversity, trauma, tragedy, threats, or significant sources of stress—such as family and relationship problems, serious health problems, or workplace and financial stressors. As much as resilience involves 'bouncing back' from these difficult experiences, it can also involve profound personal growth."[38] Do you see how much of a reality it is for you to win in life? Do you see how much of a reality it is that you *can* live unconquered? The absolute center of this approach is an unshakeable faith, a relationship with Jesus, and a life surrendered to God. That is how we can bounce back, overcome, and come back stronger and more resolved in the face of conflict.

We develop an uncommon resolve when we prioritize relationships and make an effort to take care of ourselves in every way, mind, body, and soul. If you've attempted and failed at anything in life, if you've experienced complete and total disaster but you're still going forward, you're winning. Living unconquered doesn't mean you're not going to face conflict, and it doesn't mean trouble won't come; it means that even if trouble does come, you win. It means that no matter what happens, you choose to fight and win. You choose to live. It is essential that, in this moment, you make a commitment to persevere, endure, and strengthen and equip yourself.

How we respond to the pain, crisis, and trials of life will determine our path in life. Today, Houston shares his story of surviving an injury to his face from a shotgun blast at point-blank range and how he has overcome the physical, psychological, and spiritual battles since. He left me with a quote: "You can overcome anything, period. You can come out stronger! I am thankful for every situation, and I've forgiven the man who tried to end my life that January day. I am thankful for my wife and my Savior."

Houston graciously provided me with an hour-long interview and permission to share his story here, under one condition. He asked me to share three verses with you that have been his go-to verses since January 6, 2015.

May you apply these as you develop an uncommon resolve in the face of adversity:

- "Have I not commanded you? Be strong and courageous. Do not be afraid; do not be discouraged, for the LORD your God will be with you wherever you go" (Joshua 1:9 NIV).
- "Naked I came from my mother's womb, and naked I will depart. The LORD gave and the LORD has taken away; may the name of the LORD be praised" (Job 1:21 NIV).
- "The LORD will fight for you; you need only to be still" (Exodus 14:14 NIV).

## Uncommon Resolve Requires Uncommon Unity

I don't want you to hear just *my* story. You need to know how it is possible to live unconquered. We could fill a library with books about the stories of men and women who have overcome some of the worst conflict and adversity, some unfathomable. I strongly believe we can learn from history and the experiences of others who have overcome adversity; we are fools if we don't learn from them.

What is it about men and women who face unspeakable tragedy and come out stronger, more resilient? What are the common factors that they share that we can learn from and strive to develop? It's a decision they made long before the battle began. Houston shared how he had experienced tragedy and pain prior to his shooting, and he was required to have a level of strength uncommon to many. My story isn't the only one, and neither is Houston's. *You* can live unconquered with an uncommon resolve if you prepare yourself to make that decision in the moment of truth.

If you are in a conflict right now, it's not too late to make that decision. Say it out loud: "Nothing in this world will defeat me! I will never quit the fight!" Make the decision. How do you keep going? Keep your feet moving. Head down, eyes up, ears open, mouth speaking the praises of the warrior King.

You must make the decision to continue with each breath, with each step; you may have to slow your stride, but keep your feet moving through the rounds firing around you.

This is not a battle for a lone ranger. If you want to develop your uncommon resolve in the face of temptation, conflict, or battle, it is a necessity that you see there are others who are ready to fight with you, side by side, armed and loaded.

Recite this in your head or out loud, write it down, print it off, put it in your office or home:

I decide now, and with every breath, so help me God, I will not give up the fight. I will not surrender or back down, and I will live unconquered. No pain, no past mistake, no sin, nothing in this world will control me. I serve an undefeated King, and I live unconquered!

When I am on the road speaking to audiences, primarily law enforcement, I have a unique ending and a specific reason I use it. I always share the story of a five-year-old boy hiding in a closet, with his body covered in blood and bruises, and tears are streaming down his face from absolute terror. But because he is only five, he does not know how we are supposed to pray, so he mustered up what he could: "God, send me an angel and help me out of this pain!" There's a little boy, a little girl, in every community in the United States of America experiencing sexual abuse, physical abuse, or verbal abuse. Whom do you think God will use to answer that child's prayer?

Well, I know God provides; however, I've never seen an angel with wings although I believe they exist. But, in the same sense, I've never seen a demon with horns and a pitchfork tail. God doesn't print money, and he doesn't generally send an angel with wings. However, what he will use is willing men and women, armed with experience and tools, compassion and courage, to respond to that little boy or little girl in need. Their act of desperation leads to a response from men and women behind the badge who will rescue them from horrible atrocities and get them on a path to healing.

You tell me: Are they worth fighting for? Are those men and women worth fighting for? If you are one of them, is it worth fighting for your brothers and sisters and for those hurting in your community at the hands of evil human beings? Absolutely they are worth it. And whether or not you serve as a first responder in law enforcement, firefighter, EMT, dispatcher, or service member in our armed forces, you are empowered to inspire the oppressed and hurting. You are empowered to rescue those who are having their worst day.

Just like human beings allow evil to be their influence and guide, you and I can make the decision that we are surrendered and submitted to the winning side and to be used by God for good in this world.

## Everyone Can Do Something

In our book *On Spiritual Combat*, my coauthor, Lt. Col. Dave Grossman, and I wrote about the various evils of humanity and how we can approach that battle in the spirit.

> You can think of this like the United States during World War II. The entire nation was focused on winning that war. The farmer in the field and the clerk in the store were striving, working in their jobs with victory in mind. They bought war bonds. The students in school wrote letters to our troops, collected scrap metal, and bought "war saving stamps." Every other citizen, everyone in between, accepted war rationing, and they all worked together for victory, leading ultimately to the troops in the front lines. All of them were part of a concerted effort to defend our nation and defeat our enemy.
>
> In the same way, every believer in Christ is part of a similar, vast endeavor, striving toward a single goal. In World War II we won, in large part, by killing the enemy. In this war, we win by saving lives![39]

Big battles require relentless effort, a united front, and uncommon resolve. And friends, in these times, we need all hands on deck. That's the reason I have poured my heart and soul into this book. We desperately need qualified, good, noble, and courageous first responders and servicemen and women, or, as Grossman coined them, America's sheepdogs. These are men and women who are fueled by perfect love and empowered to stand in the face of evil and say, "Not today. Not on my watch!"

If you spend any time reading the news, you know it's not good. In fact, there's seldom good news on the news. There are wars or rumors of wars; there's pure evil running rampant, corruption around the globe, and injustices that touch every part of humanity. It may seem daunting. It *is* daunting, and while it seems evil outnumbers the good, while it seems the enemy has his upper hand on the world, there's something every one of us can do.

According to a 2015 Pew Research Study,[40] 70.6 percent of Americans professed the Christian faith. If nearly two-thirds of Americans are Christian—no matter the denominational affiliation, no matter the "decline of Christianity" that some report—we have hope. We have hope because of Christ, but we have been assigned here, in this moment, for a purpose. And if our only purpose is to pray, and I mean fervently, effectively pray, then there is no greater purpose. We are the ones who will stand in the gap for the sheepdog who does battle against the wolf seeking to kill, steal, and destroy. We will be the generation who, when faced with the giants of evil in this world, did not back down.

If you are called to duty, then train, suit up, and handle your business.

If you're a law enforcement officer, serve with integrity, courage, and professionalism.

If you're a firefighter, serve with relentless courage and face the fires with hope.

If you're a member of the American armed forces, know we have your back here at home.

And if you aren't called to fight the battles of our world, you still have a role to play and a duty to fill: *pray.*

Pray fervently and pray with purpose. Pray, then act.

Think about the sacrifices made for our lives and our way of life. Jesus paid it all. About seven thousand US Armed

Forces service members have died in the War on Terror since 2001,[41] and an average of more than one hundred fifty officers are killed in the line of duty annually. That's what has been sacrificed for our way of life. Those are men and women who exemplify "no greater love."

Think about the life of NYPD Port Authority officer Christopher Amoroso. He was killed while rescuing other people from the towers on 9/11. You may recall the iconic image of Officer Amoroso, the bloodied face, a countenance of sheer exhaustion, and the heroic actions of him and many others. Their sacrifice must be known. That's the fabric of American freedoms, which every sheepdog fights to uphold. The fabric of human life, given for you, for me, whether we believe the same beliefs, whether we agree or disagree. But the common thread in that fabric is a life lived in love.

As Grossman would say here, "Sometimes the greatest love is not to sacrifice your life but to live a life of sacrifice." This is the way of the unconquered, and it is for these reasons that we must effectively, strategically, and relentlessly pray for our nation and for those who fight to defend her within the borders at home and abroad. This is why we must become vessels committed to carrying the love of Jesus wherever we go, to whomever we meet.

## Whatever It Takes...Whatever. It. Takes.

In a first-person account of his phenomenal story, Lt. Commander John S. McCain III shared how communicating with other prisoners of war was vital for survival. In times when uncertainty abounds, when lives are in upheaval, we can look at the stories of American heroes, and the story of the late Senator McCain provides invaluable lessons on surviving overwhelming odds. In his article for *U.S. News & World Report,* he said, "Communication was vital for survival." McCain wrote, "As far as this business of solitary confinement goes—the most important thing for survival is communication with someone, even if it's only a wave or a wink, a tap on the wall, or to have a guy put his thumb up. It makes all the difference."[42]

Communicate with those you can, by whatever means necessary, however possible. It keeps you connected, and as Senator McCain said, it is "vital for survival." We must not fall into the temptation of isolation. It's easy to do, and it's comfortable at times, but it is a trap from hell. But if you find yourself in that place, battling demons no one can see, you still have a line of communication available. Call on Jesus. Cry out to him. He will come to your aid just like he did for me in that patrol car on a Sunday that changed my life forever.

Your entire life has been filled with experiences preparing you for this moment—not for defeat, not for retreat, but for victory. While others have surrendered to a life of complacency, you prepare your mind, body, and soul.

Visualize the one battle; win it. Win every time. No other option exists. Visualize victory.

*This is the way of the unconquered*, and this way prepares your mind and soul. It is to your mind and soul as rigorous physical training is to the body.

You will win now, your destiny will be legendary, and your legacy will be extraordinary.

## Today Is Your Day to Decide

After *Bulletproof Marriage* was released, Grossman introduced me to a man by the name of Marcus Luttrell. In April 2019, Marcus and his team had me on their podcast, one of the best podcasts in the country, called *Team Never Quit*. We spoke after the ninety-minute interview concluded, and it was like we had known each other for our entire lives.

Marcus and his family have hosted my family and me at their ranch in Texas, and I am incredibly grateful for his friendship. While I never had the honor of serving in our nation's military, I have been challenged, blessed, and made to be a better man because of my friends, like Marcus, Dave Grossman, and so many others. You'll never hear me say I am a self-made man. I am made stronger and better because of the people in my life.

One of the first T-shirts Marcus gave me had their Team Never Quit logo on the front and, on the back, the Team Never Quit Creed. This creed was written in his book *Lone Survivor,* which was turned into a major motion picture starring Mark Wahlberg, and reads like this:

> I will never quit. I persevere and thrive on adversity. My nation expects me to be physically harder and mentally stronger than my enemies. If knocked down, I will get back up, every time. I will draw on every remaining ounce of strength to protect my teammates and to accomplish our mission. I am never out of the fight.[43]

Marcus and his family are a lighthouse of hope and inspiration for Americans. The elements of his life can be applied in the life of any American willing to do the work, create the daily habits, and have the proper mindset.

You must develop this type of approach to life and adversity. It's a choice, and yes, you can develop an unconquered mindset if you're willing to practice it. You must, through intentional effort and daily habits, forge a steel, warrior mindset, and it is essential to overcoming adversity.

I'm not sure what you've endured in life, and I may never know all the pain you've carried. I do know this: if you've struggled with it, there's hope. If you've not had the mindset of someone who is more than a conqueror, you can begin today developing it, training your mind to believe at a deeper, more powerful level. Chances are, if we were sitting across from each other and we were being honest, you would tell me there was, at some point in your life, a time you felt defeated.

Are you a child of God? Have you been redeemed by Jesus?

You are not defeated.

You are listening to the lies of the enemy.

Consider this your moment of freedom, with every single burden and shackle being lifted.

Consider this your moment of empowerment. The switch has been flipped to the On position. Walk in the power of the Holy Spirit, assured of your eternal reward through a relationship with God through his Son, Jesus. Know that, while there will be trouble in this world, we are equipped with the Comforter. Know that, while this world is ruled by the Evil One, *greater is he who is in you than he who is in this world* (see 1 John 4:4).

It's time. It's time to equip yourself with the armor of God, the power of his Spirit, and a lifestyle of prayer so you can live forward.

Live unconquered!

No matter what!

## Unconquered Code #10

Resolve at this moment that no pain, no sin, no mistake, nothing in this world will defeat you. Your declaration today becomes *I am unconquered. In Christ I live; in Christ I die. I live unconquered; I die unconquered.*

## Battle Action Step

Write down Unconquered Code #10 and place it around your home where it is easily visible. Declare it. Embrace it. Embody it.

## Discussion

1.  What things can you do to develop an uncommon resolve in your heart and mind?

2.  How do you believe adopting this new mindset and way of life can help you further the kingdom of God?

3.  Visualize the victory. You know what defeat feels like. Begin to expect victory and describe how it feels to know you cannot be defeated, ever again.

## Prayer

*Heavenly Father, my life is yours—every victory, every battle, every healing, and every moment of pain. If you want me to do battle with you by my side, I will. If you want me to be still, I will. Either way, I place my hope in you alone and ask you to go before me. Grant me victory today and every day. Every victory brings glory to you alone. In you and because of you, I am unconquered by the things of this world; in you and because of you, I live unconquered in Christ alone. Amen.*

## CONCLUSION

# FINAL THOUGHTS ON LIFE, DEATH, AND ETERNITY

Life is precious, not like a new puppy with big floppy ears precious, but like a fine, rare jewel precious. It's so fragile, and it lasts like a vapor. One moment you are here, and the next, you are gone. Today could be it. That's not fear. That's reality. We cannot control how we were born or the family and circumstances we were born into, but we can control how we live our lives.

Will you live your life in defeat or in victory? Will you be the one known as conquered by the pain of this world and the burdens of serving, or will you be the one known as *The Unconquered*?

It's a choice.

It's a mindset.

It's a way of life.

I know so many people are apprehensive about any talk related to faith, especially about Jesus. I get it. You've been scarred by religious folks, you've been told you will go to hell for your behavior, and you have been led to believe that is how God operates, waiting on you to mess up so he can free up space in heaven by sending you to hell.

That's what the enemy wants you to believe because as long as you live in fear, you never walk in power. And if you never walk in power, you never overcome the trouble in this world.

Growing up going to church so frequently, I never *felt* "saved" or "born again" (for my friends who are not Christian, these are terms referring to the moment we surrender to Christ), so anytime the preacher would give an opportunity to "get saved," I would run to the altar for prayer.

While we can have the assurance of our salvation through an authentic relationship with Jesus, there will be times, especially for those who are called to be warriors, when you may not *feel* saved or even *feel* like a follower of Christ. That's the adversary, Satan, whispering in your ears, creating doubt, planting seeds of guilt and condemnation to throw you off course. There is *absolutely nothing* like a genuine relationship with Jesus. There is no better healing, no better Comforter, and no better friend to have walking with you through life.

Hear me out here; I am not here today because someone smashed me over the head with "You're going to hell if you don't change" talk. I am here today because, at my worst, Jesus loved me like I was at my best. At my worst, my wife loved me like I deserved it when I know I didn't.

I never understood what church folks meant when they said, "Ask Jesus into your heart." That never made sense to me. You have to understand my way of thinking as a kid, knowing my whole story. I thought, *How does Jesus live in my heart? It's only taking up one part of my body. Is Jesus that small?*

No, that's not what it means at all. It means we make a *decision* to no longer live a life of misery, burdened with the things of this world. It means we recognize there is a better way, and yes, he is our Redeemer. With our human mind, using our gift of free will and choice, we *choose* to believe in Jesus. Not because we have figured it out or have a deep theological understanding of who he is or what it means to be a follower of Christ but because of faith. My prayer in the patrol car that Sunday went something like this: "I don't understand it, and I can't make sense of it all, but if you can do anything with my life, you can have it."

But we cannot stop at merely choosing to believe. Even demons believe. And Satan knows Scripture better than any preacher you have ever known, better than any theologian you have ever known. The difference is, the demons never allowed Jesus to change them, and they tried to be their own gods.

It's a choice. It's a decision. It's a process of saying daily, "Jesus, I cannot do this without you. Thank you for forgiving me, for healing me, for leading me. Thank you for redeeming me." And maybe today, your heart is hardened by the pain and grind of life. I want you to know how familiar I am with that place you are in. You don't have to figure it all out. And you don't have to have all the answers. Your unconquered life begins like this: *Jesus, I don't know what to pray, and I am not sure how to make sense of all of this. But, if you can do anything with my life, you can have it. I choose to believe. I surrender to you. Lead me!*

The day Jesus thwarted my suicide was the day I was given a new assignment. That assignment was to help others experience the love he showed me, through whatever means I could, and it became through writing and speaking. I want you to know how cynical and hard-hearted I was, how I tried to analyze and figure God out. You can stay there, like I was, and be miserable and tired all the time, or you can ask him to lead you today.

# NOTE FOR MY BROTHERS AND SISTERS IN LAW ENFORCEMENT

I would be honored to have the opportunity to share more with you about what it means to live unconquered. My heart's desire is for anyone who will take the time to read this to see what the Lord has done for me and what my mission in life is now. I do not care about your denomination affiliation. I do not care which translation of the Bible you read, and I do not care if you have tattoos or piercings or if you dress up or wear casual clothes. I do not care if you have made horrible decisions in the past. In fact, I know many who read *Behind the Badge: 365 Daily Devotions for Law Enforcement* have never gone to church or opened a Bible. That does not matter here. I love you, right where you are. I care about you, your family, your career, and your future. I want you to win, and I want you to walk this life of the unconquered. Sharing my vulnerability and pain is worth it if it empowers you and strengthens you. Most importantly, it is worth it if it leads you to discover this perfect love of Jesus and if you allow it to change your life.

You *can* live unconquered. You *can* overcome the troubles of this life. We know this world is ruled by the Evil One, but greater is he who is in *you* than he who is in this world! If that doesn't light your rocket, I don't know what will.

Cowards don't go to heaven. Fight like hell.

Live unconquered!

—Adam

# READY FOR ANYTHING

In the dark, the wolf awaits.
He seeks to prey upon those who are living their lives,
those innocent, those helpless, those who are not
     expecting his attack.
I am a sheepdog, a trained guardian of my commu-
     nity, and today,
I stand ready, prepared, mentally sharp.
I know there will be dangers and threats,
but nothing will be stronger than I am.
My past experiences have taught me I am not only a
     guardian for the innocent
but also a warrior against the violent.
My mission is clear, and I am committed to uphold-
     ing the
laws of my country and adhering to the ethics laid
     before me.
My training and experience have prepared me for
     anything I will face.
There is nothing that will stop me from apprehending
     the criminal.
I have made my decision, and I will remain focused
     on the mission,
and it is a mission to serve those in my community.
This mission isn't about me; it isn't about awards; it
     isn't about recognition.
It's about saving lives, protecting property, and appre-
     hending the
criminal who seeks to destroy innocence.
My community depends on me, and I am prepared to
     stand guard
and battle on their behalf until my last breath.

# CONDITION YELLOW

I am alert, aware, and present of mind.
I respond to victims with compassion,
to suspects with fairness and justice.
I do not permit my emotions to rule my day.
My surroundings are clear, and I do not
permit distractions to lead me to make costly
    mistakes.
I am not hypervigilant, but I am prepared to
engage any threat that may arise, and I remain alert at
    all times;
my mind is sharp, and my eyes are open.
No matter my circumstances, no matter the service
    call, I am aware.
My eyes watch the hands of those I encounter.
My ears hear the words of the victims, the statements
    of the suspects.
I have keen discernment and do not get lured into
    tunnel vision.
Today, I choose to influence those I encounter
in my life, with excellent service, and in the event
I cannot deter violence or deescalate another person,
I am prepared to engage with superior, righteous
    violence.
I remain mentally and physically sharp,
with my eye on the goal of maintaining and restoring
    law and order.
When a stressful situation arises, I will remember my
    training.
My emotions will not dominate my decision-
    making ability.
I am a sheepdog, unconquered and true.

# ACKNOWLEDGMENTS

They say writing is lonely. I suppose it is if you never listen to all the voices in your head.

There are so many people I need to acknowledge.

Thank you to the beta readers who were kind and brutal.

Thank you to Mr. Alan, my neighbor who is also a Vietnam veteran. He was kind enough to give me ruthless feedback. His wisdom is a beacon of hope in an age of ignorance.

To my retired law enforcement neighbors, thank you for your friendship, love, support, and for literally having my back. Thank you for walking with me through this journey and encouraging me.

Thank you to my pastor, Mack Ballard, for his love and leadership. He's a former cop and a chaplain to my brothers and sisters in blue! Thank you, Pastor Mack.

Thank you to those who endorsed this book for your unwavering support and for always telling me, "Don't you quit what you're doing!"

Thank you to the team at BroadStreet Publishing. Without you, we couldn't reach the world.

Thank you to my friend Marcus Luttrell. He's a friend who won't accept excuses, and because of it, he has made me a better man. Surround yourself with people who don't listen to your excuses. Also, thank you for calling me "the redneck cupid." I appreciate that.

Last but not least, my wife, Amber. You are my sweetheart, my best friend, my partner, and the one I want to grow old(er) with. You are my secret weapon, quiet but so powerful. Your support and love have made me a better man, a more confident writer, and together, we will continue to touch lives. Thank you for pushing me to keep on.

# ENDNOTES

1   "The Battle of Peleliu," Marine Corps University, accessed April 27, 2022, https://www.usmcu.edu/Research/Marine-Corps-History-Division/Brief-Histories/Marines-in-World-War-II/The-Battle-of-Peleliu/.

2   "Clearing WWII's Explosive Legacy in the Pacific," *Bangkok Post*, August 11, 2014, https://www.bangkokpost.com/world/426177/clearing-wwii-explosive-legacy-in-the-pacific.

3   E. B. Sledge, *With the Old Breed: At Peleliu and Okinawa* (New York: Presidio Press, 2007), 52–53, Kindle.

4   Epictetus, *Discourses*, trans. George Long (London: George Bell and Sons, 1890), http://data.perseus.org/citations/urn:cts:greekLit:tlg0557.tlg001.perseus-eng1:2.

5   "Trauma," American Psychological Association (website), accessed December 4, 2021, https://www.apa.org/topics/trauma.

6   David Finkelhor et al., "The Lifetime Prevalence of Child Sexual Abuse and Sexual Assault Assessed in Late Adolescence," *Journal of Adolescent Health* 55, no. 3 (September 2014): 329–33.

7   "Children and Teens: Statistics," RAINN (Rape, Abuse & Incest National Network), accessed November 6, 2021, https://www.rainn.org/statistics/children-and-teens.

8   "How to Manage Trauma," The National Council for Mental Wellbeing, February 4, 2022, https://www.thenationalcouncil.org/wp-content/uploads/2022/02/Trauma-infographic.pdf.

9   Jayne Leonard, "What Is Trauma? What to Know," Medical News Today, June 3, 2020, https://www.medicalnewstoday.com/articles/trauma.

10  Leonard, "What Is Trauma?"

11  Leonard, "What Is Trauma?"

12  "Chapter 3, Understanding the Impact of Trauma," *Trauma-Informed Care in Behavioral Health Services* (Rockville, MD: Substance Abuse and Mental Health Services Administration, 2014), https://www.ncbi.nlm.nih.gov/books/NBK207191/.

13  Evan Owens, "What Would Jesus Say to Someone Struggling with PTSD?," REBOOT Recovery, October 25, 2016, https://my.rebootrecovery.com/what-would-jesus-say-ptsd/.

14  Paulo Coelho, *The Zahir: A Novel of Obsession*, trans. Margaret Jull Costa (New York: HarperOne Perennial, 2021), 2435, Kindle.

15   Maxime Lagacé, "100 Future Quotes to Expand Your Perspective," WisdomQuotes, last modified March 6, 2022, https://wisdomquotes.com/future-quotes/.

16   John Bevere, "Multiplication | John Bevere | Sunday Night Service," Jesus Image Church, streamed live on January 30, 2022, in Orlando, FL, YouTube video, 2:48:37, https://www.youtube.com/watch?v=JIGR13yVfFk.

17   Dr. Annie Tanasugarn, "Healing from the Past and Living in Your Present," Psych Central, April 6, 2020, https://psychcentral.com/lib/healing-from-the-past-and-living-in-your-present#1.

18   "How Box Breathing Can Help You Destress," Cleveland Clinic Health Essentials, August 17, 2021, https://health.clevelandclinic.org/box-breathing-benefits/.

19   Martin Luther King Jr., *A Gift of Love* (Boston: Beacon Press, 1963), 46, Kindle.

20   "Forgiveness: Your Health Depends on It," Johns Hopkins Medicine (website), accessed January 5, 2022, https://www.hopkinsmedicine.org/health/wellness-and-prevention/forgiveness-your-health-depends-on-it.

21   "Forgiveness: Letting Go of Grudges and Bitterness," Mayo Clinic (website), November 13, 2020, https://www.mayoclinic.org/healthy-lifestyle/adult-health/in-depth/forgiveness/art-20047692.

# Endnotes

22 Dale Carnegie, *How to Win Friends and Influence People* (New York: Simon & Schuster, 2010), 74.

23 "Human Trafficking: What Is It?," Source MN Inc., accessed October 22, 2021, https://sourcemn.org/human-trafficking/.

24 "Human Trafficking," Migration Data Portal, last modified May 6, 2021, https://www.migrationdataportal.org/themes/human-trafficking.

25 Neringa Antanaityte, "Mind Matters: How to Effortlessly Have More Positive Thoughts," TLEX Institute, accessed June 10, 2021, https://tlexinstitute.com/how-to-effortlessly-have-more-positive-thoughts/.

26 "Proverbs 4:23," Bible Hub, accessed September 20, 2021, https://biblehub.com/lexicon/proverbs/4-23.htm.

27 The MacArthur Study Bible, (Nashville, TN: Thomas Nelson, 1997), 1828.

28 Michael M. Phillips, "A Stolen Boy, an Angry Loner, an Underground Bunker," *The Wall Street Journal* (website), accessed June 4, 2021, http://graphics.wsj.com/hostage/.

29 John Donne, *Donne's Devotions* (Oxford: D. A. Talboys, 1841), 195.

30 Helen Keller, *The Story of My Life*, ed. John Albert Macy (New York: Doubleday, Page, 1903), 203.

31  Robert Kurlwich, "Which Is Greater, the Number of Sand Grains on Earth or Stars in the Sky?," NPR, September 17, 2012, https://www.npr.org/sections/krulwich/2012/09/17/161096233/which-is-greater-the-number-of-sand-grains-on-earth-or-stars-in-the-sky.

32  Simon Sinek, David Mead, and Peter Docker, *Find Your Why: A Practical Guide for Discovering Purpose for You and Your Team* (New York: Penguin, 2017), 26.

33  Maxime Lagacé, "100 Discipline Quotes to Create Order in Your Life," WisdomQuotes, last modified March 10, 2022, https://wisdomquotes.com/discipline-quotes/.

34  "How We Form Habits, Change Existing Ones," ScienceDaily, August 8, 2014, www.sciencedaily.com/releases/2014/08/140808111931.htm.

35  Anna L. Boyden, *Echoes from the Hospital and White House: A Record of Mrs. Rebecca A. Pomroy's Experience in War-Times* (Boston: D. Lothrop, 1884), 61.

36  Sun Tzu, *The Art of War*, trans. Thomas Cleary (Boston: Shambhala Publications, 2011), 62, Kindle.

37  Houston Gass, "Hard to Kill: Houston Gass," BenShot, June 3, 2020, https://benshot.com/blogs/hard-to-kill/hard-to-kill-houston-gass.

38  "Building Your Resilience," American Psychological Association (website), last modified February 1, 2020, https://www.apa.org/topics/resilience.

39  Lt. Col. Dave Grossman and Adam Davis, *On Spiritual Combat: 30 Missions for Victorious Warfare* (Savage, MN: BroadStreet Publishing, 2020), 108–9.

40  "Religious Landscape Study," Pew Research Center, accessed September 3, 2021, https://www.pewforum. org/religious-landscape-study/.

41  "U.S. Military Casualties: OCO Casualty Summary by State," Defense Casualty Analysis System, accessed May 24, 2020, https://dcas.dmdc.osd.mil/dcas/app/ conflictCasualties/oco/svc/all.

42  John S. McCain, "John McCain, Prisoner of War: A First-Person Account," *U.S. News & World Report*, January 28, 2008, www.usnews.com/news/ articles/2008/01/28/john-mccain-prisoner-of-war-a-first-person-account.

43  Marcus Luttrell, *Lone Survivor: The Eyewitness Account of Operation Red Wings and the Lost Heroes of SEAL Team 10* (Boston: Little, Brown, 2007), 7.

# ABOUT THE AUTHOR

Adam is a former law enforcement officer and has faced many of the challenges law enforcement officers face daily.

In 2015, he devoted his life to delivering proven tools and resources for the mind and soul to first responders after serving in law enforcement.

His raw, unfiltered story of overcoming the trauma of childhood sexual abuse, experiences from law enforcement, and battle with suicidal thoughts and substance abuse position him as a powerful force of hope for millions of people today. His work has touched over one hundred thousand lives since 2018, and he is best known for his work to deliver faith, hope, and love to those who serve.

He has presented for major universities, law enforcement agencies, military bases, and conferences nationally.

Adam has presented his story of conquering some of life's most smothering battles and how these principles can be applied in every life to achieve optimal performance and fulfillment.

Adam's work has been featured in *Entrepreneur* magazine, Fox News, *The Huffington Post*, PoliceOne.com, and Law Enforcement Today.

His media appearances have included *The Rick & Bubba Show*, TheBlaze Radio Network, *FamilyLife Today*, *The 700 Club*, *The Glenn Beck Program*, *Team Never Quit* podcast with Marcus Luttrell, and many others.

Adam is the spokesperson for REBOOT Recovery First Responders, a nonprofit organization that focuses on providing faith-based trauma healing for first responders and service members.

He is a bestselling author with Lt. Col. Dave Grossman of the 2019 Christian Book Award Finalist *Bulletproof Marriage*.

Adam and his wife, Amber, reside with their three children in Alabama.

His sole purpose is to help others discover the life-changing love of Jesus and live a life unconquered in Christ alone.

It is a good thing to look around in the midst of the battle and see that you are not alone. A fellow soldier, one who is well-armed and fierce in his opposition to the enemy, is right there beside you. That's why we love finding that we are on the front lines with men like Adam Davis. Adam's plea is simple: don't ignore the pain of living in this broken world. Cry out to God. Plead with him to make you desperate for him. Dump it all in his lap. Seek intimacy with God, and pray that he will align your will with his. As two of Adam's fellow soldiers in the kingdom of God, we recommend this book to anyone who seeks more, anyone who desires to be liberated from the chains of bondage that we have allowed the enemy to wrap around us.

**Al and Phil Robertson**, stars, A&E's *Duck Dynasty*;
cohosts, *Unashamed with Phil & Jase Robertson* podcast

*Unconquered* is Adam Davis's best book yet and one of the most intense, empowering Christian inspirational books ever written! God has used Adam to touch vast numbers of lives over the years with his best-selling books, and his skill and maturity as an author have reached new heights. He has truly brought it all together in this book. How to forgive? Answered! How to police your thoughts? Answered! How to win the first battle of every day? Answered! How to move on from hurt to unconquered spiritual maturity and triumph? Answered! It's time to take the Unconquered Challenge.

**Lt. Col. Dave Grossman**, author and coauthor, *On Killing,*
*On Combat, On Spiritual Combat, On Hunting,*
*Bulletproof Marriage,* and *Assassination Generation*

*Unconquered* is an incredible resource not only for first responders and service members but for anyone who wants to crack the code of living a victorious life. I'm honored to endorse my friend Adam and his book *Unconquered: 10 Principles to Overcome Adversity and Live above Defeat*.

**Chad Robichaux**, founder, Mighty Oaks Foundation;
author, *Unfair Advantage* and *Fight for Us*

I personally know the pain of catastrophic failures in my life, and knowing how to apply these principles is one of the reasons I continue fighting and pressing forward. Adam's vulnerability and authentic approach to sharing deep, painful experiences teach us that no matter what we face, our past doesn't define us, we can overcome, and we can live unconquered. I highly recommend and endorse Adam and his new book *Unconquered: 10 Principles to Overcome Adversity and Live above Defeat.*

**Tim Kennedy**, author, *Scars and Stripes*

Every time I read one of Adam's books, I have to remind myself he doesn't have a background in mental health and psychology because he seamlessly integrates research-based information, psychology, and spirituality to help any reader understand a sound and direct approach to healing with God's help. *Unconquered* is the story and a guide for moving through trauma and adversity and shedding the negative influence they can have on our lives. This book has grit because Adam has the courage to share his own personal stories of trauma, struggle, awakening, and triumph. I really could not put this book down and found myself highlighting something in every chapter. If you are feeling alone and tired of the weight from situations in the past, not only will this book help you feel seen, but it will also move you through to a place of living life unconquered.

**Cyndi Doyle**, LPC-S, NCC, CDWF, CCISM, psychotherapist; founder, Code4Couples

I wish I'd had Adam's insight when trauma and tragedy met me. This book holds powerful insight you will want to have when you face any level of adversity. The introduction alone is packed with enough punch to disrupt the flow of learned helplessness. From there, it is game on.

**Barb Allen**, author, *Front Toward Enemy*; cofounder, The Great American Syndicate

All I can say is *wow*! Adam had my attention in the first chapter, and I could not stop reading. The way he openly shares about pain, trauma, and healing truly sets the stage for how to live life unconquered. *Unconquered* will teach you how to fight and come out on the other side without being defined by your past. This book and the principles it contains are going to help thousands.

**Rebecca Lynn**, author and blogger, *Proud Police Wife*

Adam captures the very essence of the term *unconquered* in this heartfelt piece. Many of us have trials and tribulations within our souls' fabric, which can often help guide others to a path of victory. Adam has mastered the courage to face fears. He also possesses the empathy to connect to generations, and he has honed the gift of articulation, translating thoughts into practical application. I proudly endorse Adam and his latest book, *Unconquered: 10 Principles to Overcome Adversity and Live above Defeat*. He is a gentleman as well as an industry professional.

**Tom Rizzo**, author, *Copikaze*

Adam writes with authenticity, transparency, and vulnerability. He has found a way to leverage pain from the past to live in the moment and recapture hope for a future. Adam's new book, *Unconquered: 10 Principles to Overcome Adversity and Live above Defeat*, is a *must* for anyone who feels defeated. These principles were birthed from personal pain and can now be used by many to fight and fight some more. We were created to live victoriously. Adam knows it, lives it, and has decided now is the time to share it.

**John Dowdey**, pastor, Church at the Crossing